W9-BVV-840

The Role of Outdoor Education

THE LIBRARY OF EDUCATION

A Project of The Center for Applied Research in Education, Inc.

Categories of Coverage

I	II	III
Curriculum and Teaching	Administration, Organization, and Finance	Psychology for Educators
IV	**V**	**VI**
History, Philosophy, and Social Foundations	Professional Skills	Educational Institutions

The Role of Outdoor Education

M. ALEXANDER GABRIELSEN

Professor of Education
New York University

CHARLES HOLTZER

Instructor in Education and
Director New York University Camp

The Center for Applied Research in Education, Inc.
New York

LIBRARY OF CONGRESS
CATALOG CARD NO.: 65–27725

PRINTED IN THE UNITED STATES OF AMERICA

Foreword

The hopes of all democracy rest on a program of education designed to develop healthy, self-disciplined, vocationally and recreationally skillful individuals who go out to meet life with scintillation and enthusiasm.

History has placed education on a pedestal. The educated man was a performer, a doer; in fact, an artist. The good citizen was one who could achieve in philosophy, music, architecture, drama, arts and crafts, or discus throwing. To be educated, in reality to be good, meant approaching perfection in performance. Education was a learning process designed for use.

The men who laid the foundation for democracy placed their hopes on universal education. Horace Mann and Benjamin Franklin predicted an enlightened, enthusiastic citizenry in which crime and delinquency would be eliminated when all men could read and write. With these tools man could dig into the educational treasures of the past and become a useful, happy citizen.

The democratic-educational train jumped the track somewhere along the line. Perhaps it was weighted down with mere numbers; perhaps educational objectives were interpreted in terms of the professions and the white-collar class; perhaps college entrance requirements were the road block; perhaps the means of education were confused with its outcomes in full living; perhaps the teachers lost faith or just got tired. At any rate, in the minds of too many, education became synonymous with that which went on in the schoolroom and with poor teaching—the *I tell you–you tell me* method. Too many teachers and parents call this kind of education "sticking to fundamentals" and therefore resist what they term the "frills" of education—music, drama, industrial arts, home economics, health, and physical education. They contend that "sticking to fundamentals" is the only way to "train the mind" and oppose methods using forums, audio-visual aids, self-government, vocational guidance, and recreation as superfluous.

This type of education leaves the masses victims of the worst phases of modern society. Those who resist crime turn to the radio, motion pictures, television, and spectator sports. We are in the gladiatorial era of Rome, ripe for a fall, not from enemies without but from an unmotivated, unskilled, bored, disillusioned citizenry.

If education cannot meet this crisis, no other social agency can be expected to fill the gap.

With few exceptions, children are being crowded into a college preparatory program; yet out of our sixty-eight million workers about ten percent will find positions in the professional or even the semi-professional group and about half of these are teachers, nurses, and hospital workers. Almost fifty percent of the entering high school group drop out before graduation because of boredom, frustration, failure, and a complete lack of interest. Any kind of work seems more attractive to these dropouts than does the free education provided by the community at tremendous expense. What would Jefferson and Lincoln have thought of our *compulsory education?*

Outdoor education represents one of the most hopeful signs of the day. It offers an opportunity for children to get out of the classroom and to learn about natural resources first hand. It exposes them to a whole cross section of educational resources about which many school books are written. The roots of the camping movement go far back into history. A Greek philosopher suggested a vacation period for the children so that they might acquire some education. David Starr Jordan sent his pupils to study "grasshopper" rather than to read about it in books. Grundtvig, the Danish poet, statesman and divine, shocked the traditional society in the Scandinavian countries in the eighteenth century by urging the establishment of Folk Schools and Peoples Colleges. The whole Folk School movement was a "learning for living" which laid the foundation for the Cooperative Movement.

It is firmly believed that outdoor education with its emphasis on significant work experience for youth, and on knowledge of the out-of-doors and community living for the younger children, offers one of the highly desirable ways to accomplish conservation results needed for the preservation of the wilderness and of the nation. At the same time, it can broaden the experience range of the total educative process; vitalize the school programs, and tie youth to the democratic group in which he lives. The outdoor education program represents a natural and desirable extension of the school curriculum. It is education.

JAY B. NASH

Distinguished Professor
Montclair State College and
Professor Emeritus
New York University

The Role of Outdoor Education

M. Alexander Gabrielsen
Charles Holtzer

An American ferment today is a reawakening in the use of the out-of-doors. While emphasis on outdoor education in our schools has recurred from time to time within the last few decades, the current stress coincides with the Federal Government's efforts to procure and improve outdoor facilities to meet increasing public demand for their use. Then, too, there is an urgent need to preserve the country's natural resources, particularly land, waterways, forests, and wildlife.

Here is an important book to assist those responsible for school programs in outdoor education. It supplies many answers to questions on the curriculum, resources, leadership, and activities and projects in outdoor education. A chapter on how to get an outdoor education program started is an invaluable aid to those who need a detailed description. From the first step of developing interest, to financing and administering the program, the processes are clear and concise.

The most essential parts of this volume are those concerned with leadership development and resources for outdoor education. The latter is a complete and up-to-date annotated listing. Descriptions are given of facilities found in virtually every area, even in those urban settings presumed to be lacking in facilities.

Throughout the book, the authors have given evidence to support current theories and practices in outdoor education. They have suggested, also, where research evidence is lacking, and what needs to be tested.

What gives uniqueness to the book is its practicality and the ease with which the reader can apply the suggestions and recommendations by the authors to virtually every educational setting.

Two competent authors combine their talents to produce this

practical, readable book. Dr. Gabrielsen, a leader in the fields of recreation, camping, and outdoor education, and in their facilities is Professor of Education at New York University. He has numerous writings in these areas to his credit, and serves as a consultant to official and voluntary agencies at the national, state and municipal levels. Mr. Holtzer makes his contributions as Instructor in Education and Director of the New York University Camp. Skilled in school camping activities, he also advises on outdoor education planning.

MOREY R. FIELDS
Content Editor

Contents

CHAPTER I

Outdoor Education and American Education

Outdoor education has been labeled by some as a product of American education in the 20th century. The statement may be true if it relates to the actual recognition by educators of the role of outdoor education in the modern curriculum, but it is a fact that man has always used nature and the out-of-doors as a learning environment. All learning had its beginning in the out-of-doors as man struggled with his surrounding environment in his efforts to survive. Today man is assuming more and more control over his environment and yet through urbanization most people in the United States have been drawn away from nature.

The desire of parents to combat the emptiness in the lives of children, resulting from the shift from rural to urban living, gave considerable impetus to the organized camping movement in this country. From a slow beginning in 1861, camping in America has grown to the point where it is an accepted part of America's culture.

Ever since the organized camping movement began in America there has been a gradual shift from camping as a charitable device for underprivileged youngsters to camping as an integral part of education. Outdoor living offers to participants many learning opportunities. Two of the most important are the development of self-reliance in people and the opportunity to put into practice many of our democratic principles.

In the days of a less industrialized America, youngsters had the fields, lakes, and woodlands as their natural environment. The rapid growth of cities began to cut away this important environment in a well-rounded life. There was a growing need to retain an awareness of nature's contributions to humanity. This need was partially met by organized camping; the 15,000 camps and 5,000,000 campers in the United States today attest to a belief in the values inherent in camping.

Mechanized urbanization has come in fast since World War II. As a result it is increasingly difficult to give America's youth the opportunities for direct learning and broad experience provided by the beauties and phenomena of nature. The restlessness of many of today's boys and girls may be partly attributed to the lack of a closeness to the land and to the wide range of learning experiences gained in a natural setting.

It has been demonstrated that learning through direct experience —by actually using nature's materials instead of merely studying about them in books—speeds the learning process, lengthens retention, and, as a result, leads to greater appreciation and understanding. Individual educational achievement in an outdoor setting is often higher than in the classroom.

A camp community illustrates the converging needs of the individual and society. For example, while undergoing experiences such as meeting all kinds of weather, preparing his own food, and living and working with members of different religions and races, the camper comes to realize that his own comfort is directly related to others and how much he must respect the rights of the other campers. Meeting the hardships of the out-of-doors often turns out to be enjoyable and leaves vivid impressions of human values.

An appreciation of our American heritage is perhaps the most important gift outdoor education and camping can give to youth. America's greatness is and always has been intimately connected with its forests, plains, and waterways. Its vast and beautiful natural resources have played a major role in the nation's development. Our long experience as an expanding country with a frontier inspired principles of individual strength of character that could be satisfied with nothing but a democratic form of government. American literature, from colonial times to the present day, has held an image of the frontier hero before every youth.

It is essential that young Americans have a chance to explore the heritage of our land, to come into contact with the soil and the treasures of the earth. T. S. Eliot, former President of Harvard University, once stated that organized camping is probably the single most important contribution of American education to the field of education; yet in spite of the recognized value of camping as an education tool, it is estimated that over seventy-five percent of all American youth never have an opportunity for such an experience.

Outdoor Education Interpreted

As the term "outdoor education" implies, it is learning away from the classroom in the out-of-doors, utilizing all the exciting resources of nature. It is accomplished through firsthand experiences involving all the senses. Outdoor education is not a new concept, but an old one which is being reinforced as a vital factor in the learning process. It does not replace classroom experiences, but supplements and enriches these experiences to make them more meaningful.

L. B. Sharp probably best stated the philosophy underlying outdoor education when he said:

> That which can best be learned inside the classroom should be learned there.
>
> That which can best be learned in the out-of-doors through direct experiences, dealing with the native materials and life situations, should there be learned.[1]

Outdoor education is not a special subject or a separate discipline. It transcends all learning, all subject matter, all disciplines, helping to make the learning process more vital and meaningful to the student. Outdoor education provides a different educational climate, one that is alive, exciting, and yields its mysteries of life and death to those who will prod into its secrets.

Koopman, in his discussion of the modern curriculum, indicates the importance of "the opportunity for growing boys and girls particularly, to be associated together in a life in the outdoors and learn the skills associated with this type of living, and learn of the habits and beauties of nature through contact with them and with the aid of organization and leadership peculiarly fitted to this purpose."[2]

Thus, outdoor education becomes one antidote for the crowded urban schools housed on limited plots of land in overpopulated cities. Schools in these settings afford little opportunity for students to assume responsibility and fulfill their inherent curiosity of the natural world around them. As Kelly pointed out:

> Some good comes from exposure to the out-of-doors because I am convinced that there is some sort of bond between the human

---

[1] *Outdoor Education for American Youth,* intro. by L. B. Sharp (Washington, D.C.: American Association for Health, Physical Education, and Recreation, 1957).

[2] G. Robert Koopman, *My Town* (East Lansing, Michigan: March, 1956).

> organism and the earth from which he sprang. We do not have scientific proof of this as yet, but we see innumerable examples of it. We feel it ourselves. There is a feeling of peace, a disappearance of life's urban problems, where one stands and contemplates a great forest, or a sunset. There is not time to multiply the many examples of what urban dwellers will do to escape into the solitude and glory of the great open spaces.[3]

Dean Brown, of Eastern Michigan State University, has vividly portrayed the value of outdoor education. He said:

> Understanding the reality and truth of the out-of-doors could serve to uncover and clarify many of the false concepts which have gone unchallenged through many years in the security, seclusion, and synthetics of the conventional classroom. The sharp challenge of the earth's surface puts to test many of those image-tools which we have only partially understood and fully misconstrued throughout long periods of time.
>
> . . . Direct personal contact may bring meaning to the many vital and intimate interrelationships which are established so clearly in nature, but which are lost in the selective, synthetic approach necessary to a restricted laboratory situation.[4]

Brown then proceeds to hit upon what may well be the most significant contribution which an outdoor education program can bring to the traditional school curriculum, the benefit which may accrue to the academic program through the medium of outdoor education. He indicates that outdoor education involves a new approach to existing, and possibly, outdated, curricular patterns and content.

> . . . [T]he teacher of academic subjects in outdoor education faces a need to review carefully one's areas of competence. No doubt, it will be necessary to re-work organized knowledge and to study further and more intensively before satisfaction or security is present. To the competent person, this is an exciting challenge. It is a far different procedure to prepare a half dozen selected specimens of either rocks, plants, or animal life than it is to walk with inquisitive and stimulated minds into an area long abandoned to nature and natural processes. One must ask oneself the purpose of the selected samples so frequently relied upon in the traditional classroom procedure. One must answer whether an educated person

---

[3] Earl C. Kelly, *Education in and for the Outdoors* (Washington, D.C., AAHPER, 1963).

[4] Albert W. Brown, "The Academic Aspects of Outdoor Education," *Extending Education,* VI, No. I.

> is one who can identify six leaves or one who understands forests. Education, in its finest sense, must be a primary goal of students and teachers in academic areas at any level.[5]

In recent years there has been an expansion of outdoor education which emphasized "educating *in* the out-of-doors" to include "educating *for* the out-of-doors." This change of philosophy emerged from the realization that individuals and family groups are turning to the out-of-doors for more and more of their recreation.

Traditionally, the outdoors has always been an important part of American life. First, as a wilderness to be conquered and then as a source of exciting, challenging recreation activities. The Outdoor Recreation Resources Review Commission Report "Outdoor Recreation for America"[6] has documented what the American people do in the summertime for outdoor recreation and projected these figures to the years 1976 and 2000. (See Table I.) To provide the areas and facilities to meet the demands of the people in the United States constitutes one of the major tasks facing this nation.

Outdoor recreation is not the same as outdoor education, although there is a close relationship. Outdoor education is school-oriented while outdoor recreation involves voluntary participation in outdoor activities such as hiking, camping, fishing, hunting, bird watching, and picnicking. To enjoy and appreciate these activities more fully an individual must possess certain levels of ability. It is in helping students acquire outdoor skills and in the development of proper attitudes and appreciation of the outdoors that the school finds its role. Thus, in the process of education for the out-of-doors the school provides the opportunity and setting for learning and practicing the basic skills of outdoor living.

Conservation education. One important aspect of preparing people for the use of the out-of-doors is the need to increase people's knowledge concerning conservation. This involves not only the preservation of open space but the wise use of the land that is available. The ORRRC (Outdoor Recreation Resources Review Commission) report points out that in one year alone (1963) over "one million acres of the American landscape was converted into sites for sub-divisions, shopping centers, highways, industrial plants,

---

[5] *Ibid.*

[6] *Outdoor Recreation for America* (Washington, D.C.: U.S. Government Printing Office, January 1962).

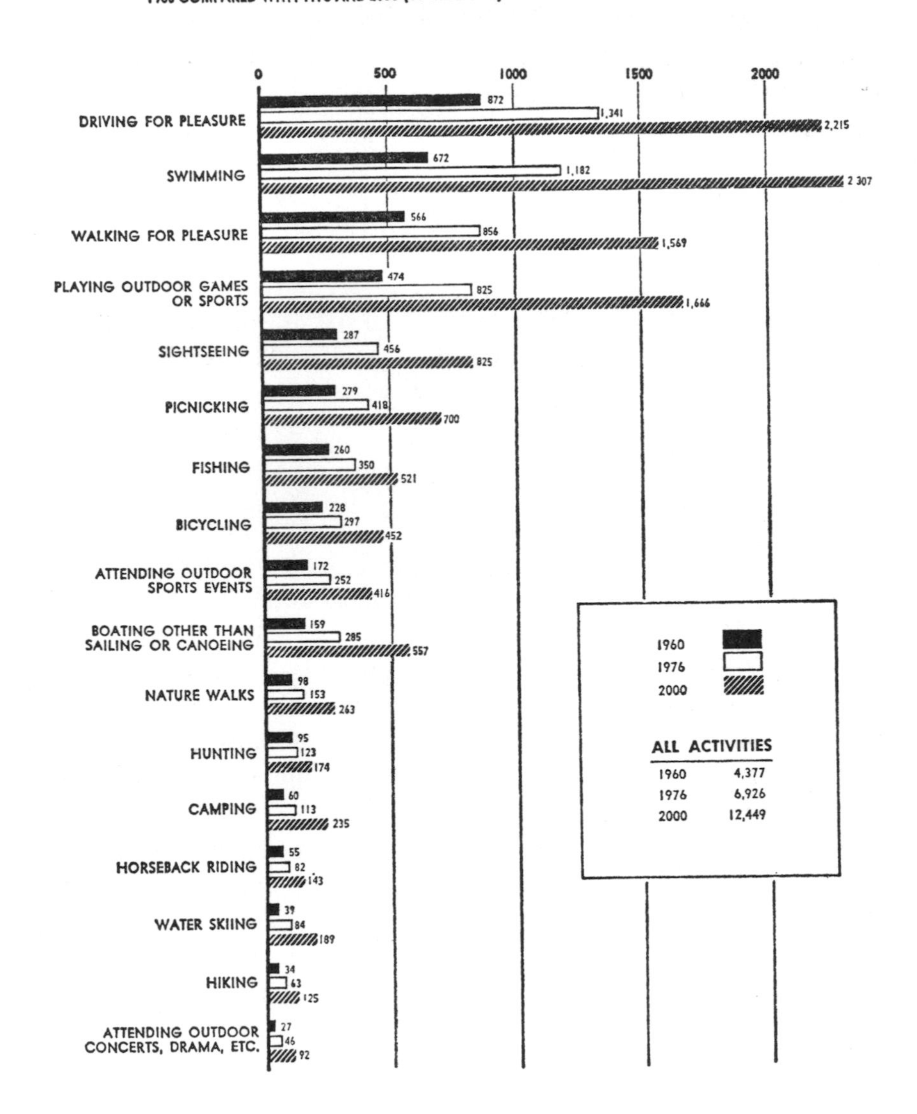

TABLE I

PROJECTION OF THE TOTAL EFFECT OF THE DEMAND FOR OUTDOOR EDUCATION FACILITIES BY THE SUMMER OF 2000

---

[7] *Ibid.*

and the other needs of an increasingly urbanized and industrial nation."[8]

Conservation is, and should be, the responsibility of everyone, including individuals, communities, and governmental agencies. Although governments at the state and federal levels possess and control much of the land it is the individual and the schools that must respond to the challenge. The need for the involvement of schools in conservation education was aptly put forth recently by a Commission of the American Association of School Administrators. They had this to say:

> The care, development, and use of natural resources in this country have been entrusted to the people individually and collectively. This widespread delegation of an important responsibility is the very essence of democratic government and is intricately related to the operation of private enterprise. The manner in which this responsibility is met depends in great measure upon a broadly conceived educational program that reaches all the people . . .
>
> School superintendents throughout the country have a deep sense of commitment for helping children and youth as well as the adult population develop the understanding and acquire the skills necessary for making effective use of natural resources.[9]

The preservation of America's wilderness. Many of man's basic needs demand open space. Alarming to many people is the rapid disappearance of much of America's wilderness areas. Highways, real estate developers, power interest, and industry are the main culprits.

America has been warned about its loss of wilderness for many years. The pioneers were Thoreau, Muir, Burroughs, and Theodore Roosevelt. Roosevelt started five national parks, fifty-one bird sanctuaries, and a vast program of reclamation projects. He actually dedicated by executive order 150,000,000 acres to our national forcst.

Much credit is also due Aldo Leopold for the direction he gave to the wilderness idea. A disciple of Leopold was Robert Marshall whose leadership gave rise to the formation of the Wilderness Society.

---

[8] Citizens' Committee for the ORRRC Report, "Action for Outdoor Recreation for America. A digest of the report of ORRRC." 1001 Connecticut Avenue, Washington, D.C., 1963.

[9] American Association of School Administrators (NEA), "Conservation in the People's Hands" (Washington, D.C.: 1964).

Roderick Nash wrote an excellent thesis on the subject "Wilderness and the American Mind."[10] He pointed out the conflict between "maintaining wilderness conditions in the face of mounting recreation needs."

There is little doubt that the preservation of America's wilderness areas will involve a continuous fight with those who want to encroach upon it in the name of progress.

The increase in leisure. Man's acquisition of more disposable time and income, the result of automation, industrialization, and the efforts of labor unions, has freed him to pursue many activities heretofore unavailable to him.

Considerable concern over this newly acquired free time has been expressed by numerous authorities. David Sarnoff sounded a warning when he said: "Not labor but leisure will be the great problem in the decades ahead. The prospect should be accepted as a God-given opportunity to add dimensions of enjoyment and grace to life."[11]

Norman Cousins in *The Saturday Review* stated:

> There still remains the biggest problem of modern man—perhaps bigger than war; what to do with himself. As he ceases to be a creature of endless toil, poverty, and famine, he is apt to be liberated into nothingness. His leisure time can become more of a curse than the plagues of old.
>
> For leisure does not carry with it automatically the birth and growth of purpose. It does not of itself make visible new horizons or lead to adventures in the fulfillment of an individual's potential. It is as neutral as the calendar. It can set the stage for meaningless distractions, expunging and consuming the awareness and the sensitiveness in man that lend him his uniqueness.[12]

No greater warning has been sounded over the concern of man's inability to cope with his newly acquired "free time" than that of the editors of *Holiday* Magazine when they said:

> One of the greatest blessings of our modern technology, and our American economic system, and of our productivity, is the new leisure they have given our people. Golden hours of one's own have been added to each day, days to each week, years to each lifetime.
>
> But the ironic, even tragic, part of this boom to good living is that practically no one has learned how to use his new leisure! The

[10] Roderick W. Nash, "Wilderness and the American Mind" (Doctoral thesis, University of Wisconsin, 1964).

[11] "The Fabulous Future," *Fortune Magazine,* January 1955.

[12] *The Saturday Review,* August 1957.

> golden hours too often become empty hours. Few of us know what on earth to do with this extra time that has been given to us.
>
> We now have the means, money, and products by which to achieve the fullest, richest life ever known to mankind, and we now have unprecedented time of our own, which might be the greatest gift of all. What we do with that gift will decide the quality, and the place in history of American Civilization.[13]

The ORRRC report on the question of whether leisure is a "blessing or curse" and the relation of man's free time to outdoor activity had this to say:

> Leisure is the blessing and could be the curse of a progressive, successful civilization. Most Americans face the prospect of more leisure time in the future, and thus the challenge of using it for their enrichment.
>
> At its best, outdoor activity is essentially a "renewing" experience —a refreshing change from the workaday world.
>
> As long as the activity is freely chosen—because it is refreshing and interesting to do—then it serves the basic function of "recreation"—the task of re-creating human vitality. Latent energy is tapped, unused powers of the body, mind, and spirit are employed, the imagination works on fresh material, and when all these things occur, the individual returns to his work with a sense of renewal.
>
> All in all, being in the outdoors is a good, wholesome, healthful use of leisure.
>
> The fact that we live in a world that moves crisis by crisis does not make a growing interest in outdoor activities frivolous, or ample provision for them unworthy of the Nation's concern.[14]

One of the most significant documents on the subject of leisure is "Leisure In America: Blessing Or Curse?" It was the outcome of a National Conference on Leisure sponsored by The American Academy of Political and Social Science and held in Philadelphia. In discussion of the values which are appropriate for the wisest use of leisure the conference report stated:

> Underlying this nation's rise to industrial prominence has been its belief in the "work ethic." The glorification of work in the "Protestant ethic," or "work ethic," has tended to produce a residual feeling of guilt toward the enjoyment of leisure for many people. If work is good, then leisure must perforce be evil. Is it not mandatory, therefore, in view of the trends predicated above, that our value system be so reoriented that the enjoyment of leisure by all be accepted as

---

[13] *Holiday Magazine,* March 1956, p. 35.

[14] Citizens' Committee for the ORRRC Report, "Action for Outdoor Recreation for America," p. 3.

> a primary value? Those who assumed the distinction between work ethic and leisure ethic generally felt that the nation had to face up to a major value reorientation if the potential benefits of increased leisure were to be realized. But there were several in the Conference who argued that this distinction was spurious, that values relating to work and leisure could be different and compatible, and that, although constructive attitudes toward leisure should be more widely accepted, it was also important to reaffirm some of the norms and attitudes usually associated with the work ethic. In other words, a person ought to be ethically responsible in all of his activities. To pose work and leisure as antithetical concepts tends to obscure the more fundamental value of personal fulfillment in all of life's endeavors.[15]

The authors of "Outdoor Education"[16] summarized the influences which have created the need for learning and living in the outdoors as follows:

1. Urbanization
2. The frenzied tempo of modern living
3. Automation and mechanizations
4. Sedentary living
5. Abstractions

These societal forces have created certain "basic human needs" say the authors which "can in part be met by outdoor education." They identify these needs as:

1. The need for creative living
2. The need for physical and mental fitness
3. The need for roots in the soil
4. The need for spiritual satisfactions

The relationship of outdoor education to the school curriculum has been described by the same authors in Table II.

The activities cited in the right hand column of the Table are examples and in no way represent a complete listing. Similarly, the list of outdoor settings for "educating in the outdoors" is only representative of the many types of settings.

---

[15] *Leisure In America: Blessing Or Curse.* Monograph 4 in a series by the American Academy of Political and Social Science (Philadelphia, Pa.: April 1964).

[16] Julian W. Smith, Reynold E. Carlson, George W. Donaldson, and Hugh B. Masters, *Outdoor Education* (Englewood Cliffs: Prentice-Hall, Inc., 1963), pp. 4–9.

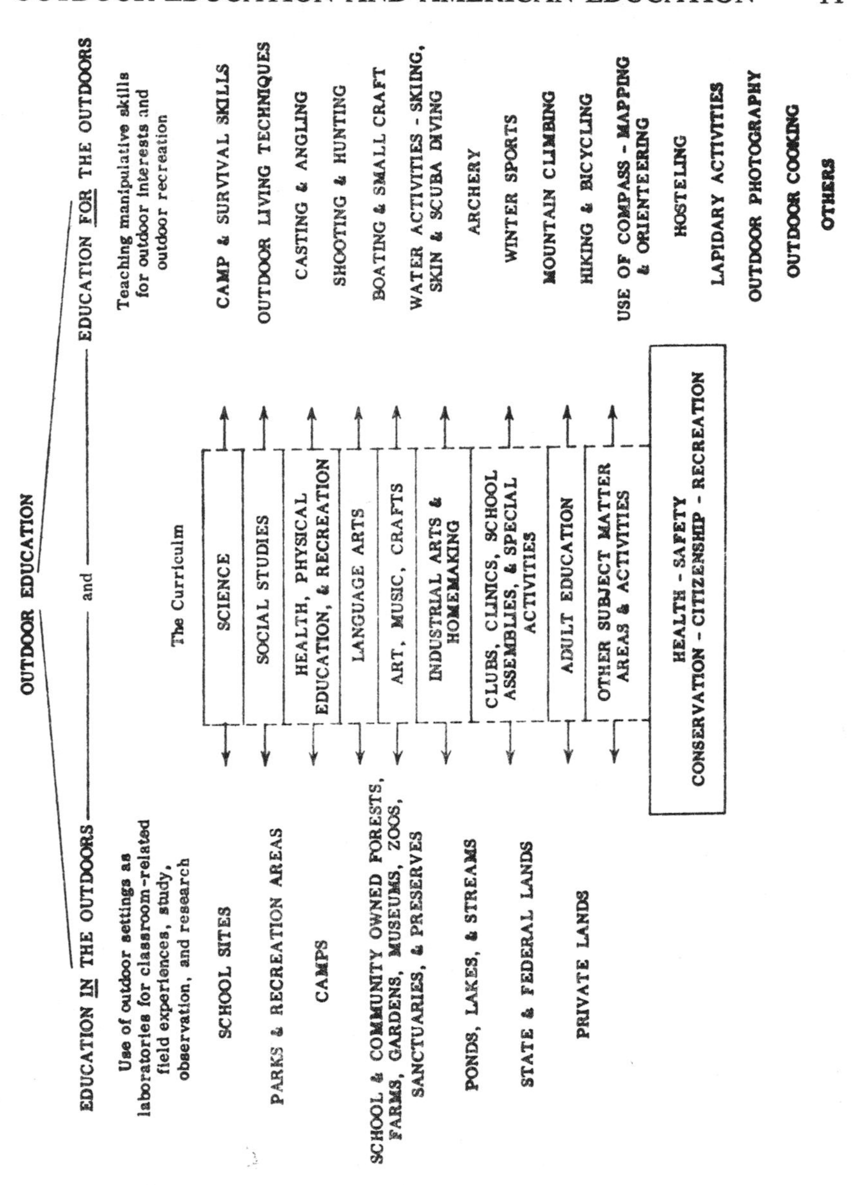

TABLE II

OUTDOOR EDUCATION IN THE CURRICULUM

[17] Smith, Carlson, Donaldson, and Masters, *Outdoor Education,* p. 17. © Reprinted by permission of Prentice-Hall, Inc., Englewood Cliffs, N.J.

Outdoor Education Nomenclature

There are many terms related to outdoor education which may easily result in confusion for some people. The definitions and interpretations that follow are designed to provide a basis for understanding.

Outdoor Education: is learning that takes place away from the classroom, usually in the out-of-doors, in subjects related to the resources of nature.

Conservation Education: is the process of learning about and developing an appreciation and respect for our natural resources in order that they continue to provide us with many of life's necessities and enjoyments. Also Leopold, one of the country's pioneers in conservation education has suggested that conservation is "a state of harmony between men and land."[18]

Wilderness: is a term that identifies a roadless region where primitive nature is modified to the least possible degree. It provides the basis for one form of outdoor life and education.

Recreation: involves activity—activity engaged in voluntarily during one's free time to provide personal satisfaction. It must not be destructive to the participant or to the society in which he lives.

Family Camping: is often referred to as "informal camping." It represents the most extensive type of camping in the United States. As the name implies it involves camping by the family unit, usually employing tents, trailers, or station wagons, and is, in most instances, conducted on public lands.

A *Camp:* is a facility in the out-of-doors which provides certain basic needs for large or small camping groups.

School Camping: is one of the components of outdoor education. It means camping sponsored by a school and conducted in a camp setting.

Camping: as defined by the American Camping Association is "an organized experience in an outdoor environment, under trained leadership, which offers campers an opportunity for growth, development, and happiness, through a program of activities related to the natural surroundings."[19]

---

[18] Aldo Leopold, *A Sand County Almanac and Sketches Here and There* (New York: Oxford University Press, 1949), p. 207.

[19] *Camping Magazine,* February 1951.

The Objectives of the Outdoor Education Program

Every program in the school's curriculum has carefully stated objectives. Although there are general broad objectives that have been developed by organizations concerned with the promotion of outdoor education programs, each school system that embarks on a program of outdoor education invariably develops its own specific aims. An examination of some fifty statements of objectives of outdoor education programs by the authors revealed a common language and general agreement on a number of specific goals. The actual words used varied somewhat but the general meaning and purposes were the same. Here is a summary and condensation of the major aims of outdoor education programs which include school camping as a major component:

1. To teach the elements of democratic living through group living, planning, and sharing.
2. To provide direct experiences in the natural and biological sciences.
3. To teach the importance of and appreciation for natural resources through realistic projects.
4. To provide the opportunity for meaningful work experiences.
5. To teach the skills involved in outdoor recreation, such as: fishing, camping, boating, hunting, and hiking.
6. To teach personal health and safety.
7. To provide the opportunity for students to assume responsibility and develop self-reliance.
8. To provide the opportunity for enjoyable fun experiences in the out-of-doors.
9. To teach survival in the out-of-doors.
10. To integrate as much as possible the outdoor experiences with the school curriculum.

Probably the two most significant sets of education goals are those established by the National Education Association's Commission on Reorganization of Secondary Schools in 1918 and the NEA's Educational Policies Commission's 1938 statement of objectives.[20] These goals have been a guide to outdoor education programming since the beginning of the movement. Properly planned and conducted outdoor education programs make a contribution to each of the seven cardinal objectives promulgated in 1918: (1) health,

[20] Alexander J. Stoddard and others, *The Purposes of Education in American Democracy* (Washington, D.C.: Educational Policies Commission of the NEA, 1938).

(2) command of fundamental processes, (3) worthy home membership, (4) vocation, (5) citizenship, (6) worthy use of leisure time, and (7) ethical character.

Some ways in which school camping may contribute to the achievement of the four basic goals of education as stated by the NEA's Educational Policies Commission is illustrated below:

A. SELF-REALIZATION

1. Through self-sufficiency in matters such as:
   - (a) Necessary personal chores, such as bed-making, care of cabin and grounds.
   - (b) Necessary personal decisions, like what clothes to wear.
   - (c) Health knowledge and habits.
   - (d) Choosing one's close friends and associates.
2. Through the discovery of:
   - (a) New and latent interests.
   - (b) Latent aptitudes and capabilities.
   - (c) The consequences of one's behavior and patterns of relationship with other people.
3. Through the development of:
   - (a) Basic skills of reading, speaking, and writing.
   - (b) Skills in sight and hearing, and recreation.
   - (c) Changed feelings and behavior in relation to people and things.
   - (d) Knowledge and appreciation of the world about them.

B. HUMAN RELATIONSHIP

1. Through experiences in peer group living, such as:
   - (a) Cooperating to help achieve group goals.
   - (b) Relating harmoniously within the group.
   - (c) Standing up against the group when the occasion demands.
2. Through experiences with campers of different groups, including those of different ages, such as:
   - (a) Mass activities.
   - (b) Interest groups and clubs.
   - (c) Spontaneous activities.
3. Through experiences with chosen friends.
4. Through experiences with the opposite sex.
5. Through experiences with authority figures.
6. Through adopting special roles, such as in:
   - (a) Dramatic activities.
   - (b) Role-playing and similar activities.
   - (c) Camper-Counselor Day.
   - (d) Serving on camper councils, as bunk captains and the like.

C. ECONOMIC EFFICIENCY

Through experiences in planning, such as:

1. Caring for limited supplies and equipment to make them last.
2. Using spending money wisely.
3. Planning menus and preparation of food.
4. Work experiences.

D. CIVIC RESPONSIBILITY

1. Through responsibilities around camp, such as:
   (a) Cleanup.
   (b) Conservation of natural resources.
   (c) Adherence to camp rules.
2. Through taking responsibility for others, by serving on camper councils and planning committees.
3. Through cooperation within a community small enough to enable the camper to see the significance of his good citizenship.

Research in Outdoor Education

Very little scientific investigation has been conducted in outdoor education and school camping. However, in the subject and activity areas related to outdoor education there has been considerable research. The ORRRC Study Report 27 contains a survey of the literature in outdoor recreation[21] which includes a partial listing of research studies. The report divides its listings into two sections; those studies and writings related to "resources"; second, those which pertain to the "user."

One of the most significant single pieces of research specifically related to outdoor education was conducted by the New York City Board of Education in cooperation with Life Camps and Life Inc.[22] The experiment involved a class of thirty students that spent three weeks at camp and a control group that remained in the city. Measurements were made in subject matter areas and personal growth with significant improvement resulting to the experimental group.

Hebel[23] and Philpott[24] studied the needs for outdoor education

[21] ORRRC Study Report 27 (Washington, D.C.: Government Printing Office, 1963).

[22] *Extending Education Through Camping* (New York: Life Camps Inc., 1948).

[23] Everett Hebel, "School Camping in New Jersey" (Doctoral thesis, New York University, 1956).

[24] Frank Philpott, "School Camping in Florida" (Thesis, New York University, 1958).

in the states of New Jersey and Florida and recommended plans for developing state-wide programs. Archard[25] developed a comprehensive plan for a school camp to serve the needs of a teacher's college and its laboratory school. Berger[26] identified the kinds of abilities and experiences classroom teachers needed prior to participation in outdoor education programs. Kleindienst[27] studied the potential experiences inherent in school camping which might supplement the education program of sixth grade pupils. Brown developed job descriptions and qualifications for camp leadership.[28]

Martha McKnight[29] studied the potential contributions of school camping. John Kirk[30] made an analysis of the laws affecting the operations of children's summer camps in the United States. In 1952 Nathan Pepper[31] conducted a study on programs, objectives, curriculum, administration, and evaluation of school camping. Esther Wenrich[32] studied the problem of staffing public school camps.

Much of the research and knowledge in the fields of educational psychology, human relations, sociology, and science have a relationship to outdoor education. There is need, however, for application of research data in these fields to the outdoor education environment. It is incumbent upon colleges and universities to encourage

---

25 Merrill H. Archard, "Recommendations for the Administration of the New Paltz State Teachers College School Camp" (Doctoral thesis, New York University, 1957).

26 Jean H. Berger, "A Plan for Developing Competencies for Leadership in School Camping and Outdoor Education for Elementary Education Students" (Doctoral thesis, New York University, 1958).

27 Viola K. Kleindienst, "A Study of the Experiences of Camping for the Purpose of Pointing Out Ways in Which a School Camp Program May Supplement the Elementary School at the Sixth Grade Level" (Doctoral thesis, New York University, 1957).

28 Jean C. Brown, "Job Descriptions and Qualifications for Camp Leadership Positions" (Doctoral thesis, New York University, 1958).

29 Martha E. McKnight, "Contributions and Potentialities of School Camping" (Doctoral thesis, Columbia University, 1952).

30 John J. Kirk, "An Analysis of State Laws Affecting the Operation of Children's Summer Camps in the United States, with a Suggested Universal Legislation Program" (Doctoral thesis, University of Michigan, 1963).

31 Nathan H. Pepper, "A study of School Camping with Special Emphasis on Program, Objectives, Curriculum, Administration, and Evaluation" (Thesis, University of Houston, 1952).

32 Esther M. Wenrich, "The Staffing of Public Elementary School Camps" (Thesis, Columbia University, 1955).

more research in outdoor education. A few of the essential questions which need scientific investigation are:

1. What is the relative effect of short term camping (one week) and long term camping (one to two months) on the social, emotional, and educational development of the child?
2. To what extent is the learning rate of different age children changed by a resident camp experience?
3. May attitude changes occur in children as a result of a resident camp experience?
4. What elements of subject matter material can best be taught in the out-of-doors?
5. Can a group camp experience change the personality of a child?
6. What are the elements in a camping experience which have a motivational effect on children?
7. What type and quality of preparation for teachers is essential to effective leadership in the out-of-doors?
8. What kind of instrument may be developed for evaluation of outdoor education programs?
9. How is an outdoor education program in a school district best administered?
10. What kind of instructional areas or facilities need to be provided in order to adequately conduct an outdoor education program?
11. What outdoor education experiences contribute most to the development of the child?

Outdoor Education's Future

The first quarter century of outdoor education has seen a gradual increase in interest by educators with sporadic experimentation of programs throughout the country. No state has yet developed a comprehensive plan for outdoor education, and in no state is there full participation by all school districts. Some of the ardent proponents of the program have expressed disappointment at the slow progress in outdoor education.

One explanation for the slow movement is that the first twenty-five years of outdoor education spanned the periods of World War II, the Korean conflict, a post-war school building boom, and a ten year teacher shortage. Another explanation is that it takes from twenty-five to fifty years for a new education concept to be fully accepted. Thus outdoor education is "on schedule."

The authors believe there are a number of obstacles to the

growth of outdoor education. They are listed here, not in any order of relative importance, to guide schools and individuals desiring to initiate and develop their own program.

1. Lack of definite policy on outdoor education by state departments of education.
2. Recognition of outdoor education as merely an appendage to one of the special subject fields such as science, physical education, or social studies.
3. Lack of appropriate legislation for outdoor education in each state to permit total effort by local school districts without fear of overstepping legal boundaries.
4. Absences of programs of outdoor education in most teacher education institutions preparing teachers to assume leadership in the out-of-doors.
5. Small school sites, particularly in high population density communities, which prevent programs from getting started on school grounds.
6. Unavailability to schools of appropriately located camp sites for resident school camping programs.
7. Lack of acceptance of outdoor education as an integral part of the educational process by school boards and administrators.
8. Paucity of research in outdoor education.
9. Attitude on the part of the public that camping conducted by schools is outside the school's curriculum and is a fad or a frill.
10. Lack of cooperation between the conservation agencies of the federal, state, and county governments, and schools.
11. Absence of enthusiasm for the program by many teachers, most of whom are untrained for participation and, therefore, feel uncomfortable about their ability to teach or perform in the out-of-doors.
12. In some instances, the demand of teachers for extra compensation for their participation in school camping programs. Teachers claim that it involves twenty-four-hour duty per day and takes them away from their families for a week or more.
13. Lack of funds for the support of local programs and for research in outdoor education.
14. Pressure placed on schools by increasing enrollments and need for new buildings which has deterred the initiation of new programs which involve additions to the school budget.

The uniqueness of outdoor education is easily identified. It is the utilization of nature's environment as a laboratory for learning. The inherent character of the outdoor environment provides a great many other learning opportunities of which democratic living is one of the most important.

The future of outdoor education, the extent to which it receives acceptance and becomes a vital force in America's educational program will depend a great deal upon how well the pioneers and experimentors do their job. As objective evidence related to the value of outdoor education becomes available, the basis for growth and approval will be established.

CHAPTER II

The Nature of Outdoor Education Programs

Whenever a teacher escorts her class from the schoolroom to the exterior of the building, she has taken the first step in the initiation of an outdoor education program. The class emerges into a completely different learning environment from the classroom, one that possesses unlimited educational opportunities. Students are free of textbooks and other conventional learning devices. The subject matter now available to them is found in the total resources of the community and surrounding area. Outdoor resources contribute to almost every aspect of living.

Conventional subject matter curriculum guides and state syllabi do not exist for the area of outdoor education. This lack has one advantage; it stimulates schools to develop their own programs. The methods and techniques employed, the scope of activities, and the multiplicity of settings for outdoor education are almost unlimited. This chapter will discuss those programs which are school-sponsored and oriented.

Excluded from this discussion are the physical education and sports programs which are also conducted outdoors. Furthermore, the traditional recess period is not included although it does afford an opportunity for participation in a variety of outdoor education activities.

Programs in the out-of-doors range from short excursions such as hikes and field trips to extended outings of up to one or two weeks. Extended programs are usually conducted at a camp where the students live, study, work, and play together.

The variety of outdoor education programs in this country that are available for schools and teachers to choose from is discussed in the sections that follow.

The Field Trip

The most common type of outdoor education program is the field trip or "excursion" as it is often labeled. Some refer to it merely as a "hike." Whatever the label, the trip must be planned, even if it is a short "look-see" type of trip, or one that takes the better part of the school day. Freeberg and Taylor[1] have an excellent chapter in their book *Programs in Outdoor Education* on the subject of "School Journeys," another name for field trips. They not only identify the activities but discuss the procedures involved in the proper conduct of such trips. Field trips are usually divided into three general categories:

> *Educational Trips:* Visits to such areas or facilities as zoos, water purification plants, sewage disposal plants, stone quarries, museums, historical landmarks, lumber mills, dairy products plants, food processing plants, battle sites, mines, nature centers, manufacturing plants, parks, reservoirs, dams, weather stations, and many other facilities unique to the locale.
>
> *Natural Science Trips:* Visits to such places as geological centers showing local rock formations, weather stations, glacial deposits, and mineral deposits, in order to learn about their general and specific relationship to the soil and plants.
>
> *Conservation Lessons:* Visits to eroded areas, fire devastated areas, forests, fire lookout stations, farms, fish hatcheries, wildlife refuges, game farms, reforestation projects, bird sanctuaries, animal or bird feeding stations, dams, and stream improvement projects to study their contributions to conservation.

Day Camping

A day camping program is having a class, or group of classes, go to a specific camping area, or an established camp site, for a full day. The group using the camp as their headquarters or base of operations carries on a program of outdoor activities. In the same camp setting lunch is usually prepared outside by the group, or in some instances a prepared lunch is brought from the school cafeteria or home.

School Camping

School camping, as the name implies, is camping under the sponsorship and auspices of a school. The term is used to identify the kind of outdoor education programs where a class or group of classes spends two or more days in a resident camp setting. The camp facility may be leased or owned by the school system, or in

[1] William H. Freeberg and Loren E. Taylor, *Programs in Outdoor Education* (Minneapolis, Minn.: Burgess Publishing Co., 1963), pp. 102–135.

some instances the school uses a facility owned by a county or a department of a state, such as the conservation department. In a few cases schools have used private camp facilities or camps owned by voluntary agencies such as the Y's or Scouts.

Although America pioneered the organized camping movement, American educational leaders have been slow to recognize the great values inherent in school camping. The states that have led the way in the development of school camping programs are California, Illinois, Indiana, Michigan, New Jersey, New York, Texas, Ohio, and Wisconsin. The early history of school camping is a little vague. Most authorities seem to agree that the program dates back to at least the year 1912 when the school board of Dubuque, Iowa initiated a summer camping program for malnourished children in cooperation with the Visiting Nurse Association. Other pioneering programs were started in Chicago (1919), Los Angeles (1924), and Irvington, New Jersey (1925). In the early 1930's Chicago, Dallas, Dearborn, Jersey City, LaCrosse, and New York saw school camp programs get started in their communities.

The first camp site operated by the Los Angeles City schools was called "Clear Creek Forestry Center." It was located in the Angeles Crest area of the Angeles National Forest and consisted of 200 acres of chaparrel covered hillsides and canyons.

By 1964 it was estimated that no fewer than 2,000 schools in the United States were involved in some form of school camping program. Half of this number are of the day camp variety.

The school camp provides the best setting for carrying on a comprehensive program of outdoor education. Almost all aspects of outdoor education may be conducted in the resident camp where children live, work, study, and play twenty-four hours a day.

The most prevalent age groups that take part in school camp programs are the 4th, 5th, and 6th grades, with more 6th grade youngsters participating than any of the other groups. The difficulty of scheduling a class at the high school level, where the students' programs vary so greatly, has prevented greater participation by that age group. Steps should be taken to solve this problem since great value may be derived by high school students from a school camping experience. One possible solution in small junior and senior high schools is to take a whole grade to camp at one time. This would enable the various subject matter teachers to accompany the students.

The School Garden

By far the most prevalent of all outdoor education programs in this country is the school garden. Almost every school in America has something growing, if not outdoors at least in pots, window boxes, or in greenhouses, if they are fortunate enough to have one in the school. The need for such activity has never been greater. It fills the gap for city children living in cold-water flats or high rise apartments. It allows teachers to make the study of botany more realistic by using living things.

The outdoor school garden located on the school grounds is emerging as an accepted facility of equal importance to the football field or baseball diamond.

To the public schools of Cleveland, Ohio goes the honor of having the best gardening program of any large urban city in the United States. Gardening is taught as a unit in science from the elementary grades through junior high school. The Cleveland school system has six greenhouses and over twenty acres of school gardens spread throughout the city. The program has been in operation for sixty years.

Other cities which have paid particular attention to gardening as a part of their school programs are New York, Philadelphia, Minneapolis, and Los Angeles. Often the school's garden program is assisted by local garden clubs or parent-teachers' associations.

An encouraging outcome of the school's gardening program is the development of home gardens motivated by what children have learned in the school's program.

A school garden varies greatly in type and program emphasis. It may be a rock garden, vegetable garden, flower bed, tree garden, nursery, indoor garden, inner courtyard garden, or greenhouse.

More schools should involve the children in planning and caring for landscaped areas around the school. Such activity would add beauty to the school while the children are learning how to plant and care for living things.

Another extension of the garden program is the beautification of the neighborhood or community through planting days. The country of Israel has national tree planting days in which school children play a vital role.

The School Forest

The least known outdoor education program is the school forest. Such a program got its start following the heavy cutting of our great forests, particularly in the midwestern states of Michigan, Wisconsin, and Minnesota. The primary purpose of the school forests was the reforestation of the land. A secondary purpose was to create a learning laboratory in the forest environment.

The most extensive development of school forests is in the state of Wisconsin. In 1927 a law was passed (revised in 1949) which authorized that "any city, village, town, or school district may acquire land, engage in forestry, and appropriate funds for such purposes. In the case of a city or village or school district, the forest property may be located outside the city or village limits."

The enactment of this law by Wisconsin's legislators stimulated many school districts to acquire land. In some instances, land was deeded to a local school system by the state agricultural or conservation departments. In other cases, the land was given free to the school by private owners.

Most states need to pass appropriate legislation permitting school districts to acquire land for school forest purposes and authorize expenditures of tax funds in the development of outdoor education programs.

Over two hundred school systems in Wisconsin own school forest tracts. In addition to reforestation the land is used for recreation and education purposes. Some of the educational activities carried on, in addition to tree planting, are: Christmas tree harvesting and sale, map preparation, developing master plans, insect and disease control, and pruning and thinning of trees. Where streams or rivers pass through or border on school forests, fish and stream management programs are also available to school children.

Schools located on adequate sites may consider starting a tree nursery. Trees thus started may eventually be transplanted to beautify the school's property. One acre of land is sufficient to initiate such a program.

School forests tend to instill in students a greater appreciation of a most valuable resource, while at the same time they contribute to an awakening of the individual's social responsibility to conserve our woodlands.

The School Farm

Ever since agriculture was introduced as a subject in the school curriculum, mostly in rural communities, school systems have owned or leased and operated farms. The farm which is used by the school strictly for its agricultural curriculum is one type of school farm. The other type is the farm operated as a part of the school's outdoor education program. The first type is for vocational development, while the second is designed to orient and educate students in the many functions and services performed by the farms of this country.

One of the drawbacks of the school's agricultural farm is that it is almost exclusively for the use of students enrolled in agriculture courses. Most school farms are owned by the school district. Others are leased or used in agreement with the owner.

The farm is an exciting place for school children to visit. There are cattle, horses, chickens, sheep, and other farm animals to see. The variety of crops can be a real attraction to students, as is the modern farm machinery used for milking cows, tilling the soil, and harvesting crops.

The two most prominent school farms operated as outdoor education centers are found in Tyler, Texas and Battle Creek, Michigan. In both of these farms children from kindergarten through high school visit the farm and many work on specific farm projects.

The experiences provided by the school farm will become more and more valuable to children as fewer and fewer people live on farms. The day might well come when farmers will welcome an arrangement with school districts whereby high school students will spend some of their free time, particularly on weekends or during vacations, helping out the farmer.

More schools should acquire, through purchase or lease, farms near their communities which could serve the needs of children for this kind of experience. It has been demonstrated that school farms can be self-supporting, and, therefore, need not be a burden to local taxpayers.

Conservation Education

Conservation is one of the major objectives of outdoor education. Considerable attention is given to conservation by various agencies of the federal government such as the Department of Agriculture, the Department of the Interior, the Tennessee Valley Authority, the Forest Service (under the Department of Agriculture), and the National Park Service (under the Department of Interior). In addition, there are numerous other agencies which are supported by voluntary contributions that promote conservation. The Pinchot Estate in Pennsylvania is being developed as a Conservation Education Center. A list of conservation agencies is listed in the appendix.

One of the most significant publications in recent years on the subject of conservation was published by the American Association of School Administrators.[2] It is an excellent statement on the need for conservation and it contains many helpful suggestions for the solution of problems in conservation education.

The Work Camp

The work camp, established for older youth, is not always identified as a part of the outdoor education program, unless it is under the auspices of the school. Although the work camp concept is quite new to America, the movement had its early beginning in Europe. In America, the Civilian Conservation Corps camps of the 1930's were excellent examples of work camps. A work camp involves a group of people, mostly youth, performing physical work involving projects which usually have some value to others. The Kibbutz's of Israel are examples of communal living where the major orientation is towards work.

Several experiments have been conducted with work camps in the United States. One of the first, for twenty-five high school boys and girls, was conducted by the Progressive Education Association with the cooperation of the Ethical Culture Schools, the Lincoln School, and the George School in 1938. The American Friends Service Committee has been conducting camps primarily for high school and college students for many years. The Hudson Guild Camp at Andover, New Jersey and the Stepney Camp at Botsford, Connecticut are other pioneer work camps.

Dr. Ernst Bulova started the first private work camp called Bucks Rock in New Milford, Connecticut. The Shaker Village Work Group at Mt. Lebanon, Massachusetts and the Lincoln Farm Work Camp in Roscoe, New York are other privately sponsored teenage work camps which have been successful.

---

[2] American Association of School Administrators, *Conservation—In The People's Hands,* 1201 16th Street N.W., Washington, D.C., 1964.

President Johnson's legislation for his War Against Poverty enacted by Congress in August 1964 includes a "Job Corps" for youth which has as one of its programs "Job Corps Conservation Camps." The primary goal of the camp is the "rehabilitation of youth for successful living." The camp program includes basic education, work experiences, and social living. They are not specifically vocationally oriented but subscribe to the thesis that through work, supervised by sympathetic adult leadership, disadvantaged youth may achieve a purpose in life and make adjustments so that they may become responsible self-reliant citizens.

The work concept need not be limited to the work camp. Every children's camp and school camp should include in their programs some work experiences for the campers. A few examples of the kind of purposeful work experiences which may be incorporated into the camp program are:

Construction projects: building docks, trails, roads, beaches, plumbing.
Repair projects: painting, boats, canoes, cabins.
Conservation: soil testing and fertility, fine clearing, reforestation, brush shelters for animals, dam construction, stream improvement, landscaping, and bird feeding station.
Farming: planting and maintaining vegetable garden, maintaining dairy herd, harvesting.

For work projects to be of value to campers there must be considerable planning and preparation before starting, there must be some guidance and leadership, and there must be follow-up and evaluation. The group that plants corn must be given the opportunity to see and pick the corn when it reaches maturity. This might even involve coming back after camp is over.

Outdoor Clubs

One of the most common school programs in outdoor education is The Outdoor Club. It may exist under several different names—outdoor science club, outing club, nature club, ski club, hiking club, and camping club. Youth hostels, which often are organized in schools, represent another type of club. In most instances these clubs have a social and recreational orientation; however, when proper leadership is provided the activities become educational as well as recreational.

Significant outdoor education programs. It is difficult to identify and list completely programs in outdoor education, since it is almost inevitable that a number of excellent programs would be overlooked. However, it is valuable for reference purposes to note the programs which have had the greatest effect on the field.

Outdoor Education Association: Early in the development of outdoor education programs the Outdoor Education Association was formed. Its founders and early leaders were Dr. L. B. Sharp and Dr. De Alton Partridge, President of Montclair State College. The organization has continued to promote the concept of learning through living in the out-of-doors.

National Camp: This was a training camp started by Dr. L. B. Sharp in 1940. It had a children's demonstration camp associated with it. Here teachers and school administrators from all over the country came to participate in summer workshops. The workshops were co-sponsored by New York University for graduate credit.

W. K. Kellogg Foundation: This foundation was one of the motivating forces in the early development of outdoor education programs in the 1930's and 1940's. It sponsored the development of several camp programs, particularly in Michigan. It also cooperated with the states of Michigan, New York, California, and Washington in the conduct of camping demonstrations and teacher education workshops.

New Jersey School of Conservation: One of the most significant programs being carried on in outdoor education is in the state of New Jersey. The division of Higher Education of the State Education Department of New Jersey created the School of Conservation at Stokes Forest. Here, each year over 4,000 students come from the New Jersey state colleges for an outdoor living experience and training in outdoor education and conservation. It is a mandatory program which requires every student, usually during the sophomore year, to participate for one week. In addition to the college students over 2,000 elementary grade pupils from the public schools of New Jersey participate in a school camping program at Stokes. Credit for this program belongs to Dr. De Alton Partridge, President of Montclair State College and Cliff Emanuelson, the school's first director. Newark State College, through Dr. Kenneth R. Benson, also has developed a program for graduate students at Stokes Forest as well as for undergraduates.

Outdoor Education Project: This project had its origin in 1955 and is a joint venture of education, industry, and professional groups. Operation of the project is under the supervision of the American Association for Health, Physical Education, and Recreation, a department of the National Education Association. The director of the project from the beginning has been Dr. Julian Smith. The major purpose of the project is to assist schools and communities in the initiation of programs of outdoor education. It also has sponsored numerous regional outdoor education workshops for teachers and school administrators, and recreation, camping, and conservation specialists.

The Tennessee Valley Authority: In January 1964, Congress authorized the Tennessee Valley Authority to proceed with the development of a 170,000 acre demonstration area known as the "Land Between the Lakes Project." The purpose of the project was to create a national recreation and camping area. The name "Land Between the Lakes" is derived from the fact that it lies between two man-made lakes, the Kentucky and the Barkley. 4,500 acres have been allocated to a conservation education center for use by schools in the area. The project could become one of the most significant outdoor education ventures in the United States. Robert Howse is the project director, and Harold Van Morgan, the chief planner, and the person who originally conceived the idea.

Northern Illinois University: In 1951 the University created the Lorado-Taft field campus. It is used essentially for the preparation of elementary school teachers in outdoor education.

Southern Illinois University: The University has developed a most interesting outdoor education center on a 1,400 acre tract of land on Little Grassy Lake. Dr. L. B. Sharp developed the master plan for the center. The center is in its early developmental stage and when completed is expected to make a significant contribution to outdoor education in that section of the country.

New York University: One of the pioneers in outdoor education and camping is New York University. In 1926 it acquired a camp, located in the Harriman section of the Palisades Inter-State Park and since then has served over 10,000 graduate and undergraduate students from every state in the Union and 42 foreign countries. The camp was developed under the inspirational leadership of Dr. Jay Bryan Nash in cooperation with the Palisades Inter-State Park Commission.

In 1962 the University acquired its own tract of land in Holmes,

New York and shifted its many camp leadership programs to that unit of the University Camp, now known as the Henry Kaufmann Center for Camp Leadership. The camp has cooperated with over twenty-five school districts in metropolitan New York in the conduct of demonstration school camping programs and has sponsored numerous workshops for school teachers and administrators. In 1949 the University initiated the first graduate program with specialization in camping and outdoor education, leading to the master's and doctor's degrees.

Michigan: The state of Michigan has developed a number of outdoor centers which are administered by the Parks and Recreation Division of the Department of Conservation. They are available to organized groups for the purpose of training children in a program consisting of conservation, outdoor recreation, and good community living. Extensive use is made of the centers by school groups as outdoor learning laboratories.

Under the leadership of Dr. Julian Smith, Michigan State University has developed courses and sponsored summer workshops for teachers in outdoor education.

Others: All of the colleges in the University of the State of New York now own or lease camps for the training of teachers and for providing outdoor experiences for their undergraduate students. Antioch College, Indiana University, Springfield College, Penn State University, and the University of Washington are other colleges that have developed programs in the field.

Communities that have been most active in outdoor education and school camping programs are Battle Creek, Pontiac, and Dearborn, Michigan; Tyler, Texas; San Diego, Pasadena, and Los Angeles, California; Scarsdale and Roslyn, New York; Minneapolis, Minnesota; Webster Grove, Missouri; Frederick County, Maryland; and Newton, Massachusetts.

Additional states that have been active in promoting outdoor education programs are New Hampshire, Florida, Ohio, and Oregon.

CHAPTER III

Outdoor Education and the School Curriculum

Value of Direct Experiences

The question has often been asked by curriculum planners, "What justification is there for incorporating outdoor education experiences into the school curriculum?" Outdoor education, as indicated previously, provides children with direct learning and living experiences in nature's outdoor setting to supplement the regular school curriculum.

In today's ever-changing, complex world it has become increasingly necessary for educators to re-evaluate, modify, and in some instances radically change the school curriculum and methods of teaching in order to meet the demands of more broadened educational responsibilities. Adjustment to life is becoming a more important responsibility of formal education. As "man cannot live by bread alone" so man cannot live by books alone. "Learning by doing" is the philosophy fundamental to outdoor education and is a vital part of the educational process.

There are many different types of experiences which every school child should have and which outdoor education helps to provide. They are indicated in one of the bulletins published by the University of the State of New York:

> To learn to live the good life is to learn to take advantage of a flow of experiences which include personal behavior, concentrated study, economic endeavor, appreciation of the finer things in life, happy and constructive use of leisure time, an appreciation and respect for one's country, and an enrichment of the spiritual side of life. The school camp furnishes a natural setting for the development of these qualities.[1]

Many claims have been made about the advantages obtained through integration of outdoor education within the school curricu-

[1] Physical Education and Recreation Series, "School Camping and Outdoor Education," *Bulletin,* University of the State of New York, Albany, May 1950, p. 25.

lum. A number of these claims, unfortunately, have not yet been substantiated by research. Indeed, there are some qualities inherent in an outdoor education program which cannot be subjected to scientific analysis. Although it is true that feelings can be measured scientifically, no method of psychological testing has yet been devised that manifests all of the mental ramifications involved which might result from one viewing the Grand Canyon or Niagara Falls for the first time. Such an experience may influence a child in his attitude toward nature or religion, now or in future years. It may encourage him to seek fuller enjoyment of the outdoors in years to come through an avocation such as camping or, possibly, through a vocation related to the outdoors.

There are certain experiences which may have an emotional impact on a child of far more importance than the value they may have when an explanation of a scientific nature is made. For example, reading a poem or a piece of prose about the beauties of nature to a group of children sitting on a hillside while a beautiful sunset slowly emerges may be more evocative than to point out the scientific explanation for the causes of sunsets.

In some areas, educators have based their conclusions about the value of certain outdoor education activities on their own experiences. The advantages seemingly inherent in living together with others is one of the major benefits that proponents of outdoor education claim for the program. Their claims apparently have some basis. Planning, working, learning, and living with one's peers appear to help a child adjust more readily to his social environment.

A child who is limited in his social contacts may experience difficulties in his personal development and in making social adjustments with others now and in years to come. Lindgren gave support to this claim when he wrote:

> Furthermore, through our associations with others, we learn how to express ourselves both through describing our thoughts and feelings, as well as through exercising our creatives abilities. Personal contacts and friendly relations with others are almost as essential as life itself.[2]

Jersild also lent some support to the above claim when he stated:

> An important aspect of a child's social development is his growing

---

[2] Henry Clay Lindgren, *The Art of Human Relations* (New York: Hermitage House, Inc., 1954), p. 165.

> perception or awareness of the feelings, moods and intentions of others.[3]
> The rejected child . . . is likely to feed on his rejection; the experience of being rejected is more likely to strengthen rather than remove the qualities that led him to be rejected in the first place. . . . it is likely that a child who has been rejected by his peers . . . will move into adult life with a trace of bitterness.[4]

Because a student's behavior in the classroom and, in some cases, his progress in learning can be affected by his relationships with others, social adjustment should be considered as an integral part of his education. A student cannot be divided into sections so that the teacher can conveniently concentrate on educating only one or two of the parts.

Russell contends that social or group factors may have great influence upon the level of aspiration of a child. These influences may considerably affect his approach to various problems such as school work and also affect his success in solving these problems.[5]

Consequently, educators have placed greater emphasis over the years in educating the so-called "whole child" just as more medical doctors have taken into consideration their patients' mental attitudes when treating their physical ills. Living together twenty-four hours a day in a school camp provides children with opportunities for experiences in social adjustments that are not possible in the classroom.

Some may argue that children have such living experiences in a summer camp. This is not entirely true. First, there are many children from all socioeconomic levels who never attend a summer camp and, second, the nature of the programs at summer camps are vastly different from those found in school camps. It should be emphasized that school camping *is an extension of the school curriculum.* Summer camping, except for a few specialized camps, is not.

In addition, many schools have children who come from a variety of socioeconomic backgrounds. This is often not the case in summer camps. The school child in a school camp setting often has an opportunity to live and interact with youngsters from a variety of ethnic and cultural backgrounds. School camp experiences have

---

[3] Arthur T. Jersild, *Child Psychology* (Englewood Cliffs, N.J.: Prentice-Hall, Inc., 1962), p. 203.

[4] Jersild, *Child Psychology*, pp. 211, 214.

[5] David H. Russell, *Children's Thinking* (Boston: Ginn & Company, 1956), pp. 188–189.

shown that there tends to be a greater working together for the duration of the school term among students who have been to a school camp for only one week than is obtainable in the classroom. The relationship between teacher and pupil in many instances also shows marked improvement. A teacher cannot help but get to know pupils better when living, planning, and working with them twenty-four hours a day in a variety of situations. In addition, the students get to know their teacher better. Many teachers known by the authors have testified that as a result of a school camp experience they acquired more knowledge about the general abilities of many of their students. Some slow learners, when placed in a more informal educational setting, appeared to perform much better academically. By the same token, teachers have also discovered that some bright students lack "common sense" and/or ability in manual skills. An observing teacher can take this new-found knowledge back to the classroom and use it advantageously with individual children.

Although some of the claims made for outdoor education have not been subject to research, there are values of outdoor education programs which have been objectively studied. One of the questions which requires scientific scrutiny is "Can certain school subjects be taught more effectively and with more understanding, more practical knowledge, and greater retention through the medium of the outdoors as opposed to classroom methods?" Many educators believe they can. Dean Albert W. Brown of the College of Arts and Sciences at Eastern Michigan University supported this belief when he stated:

> First, and perhaps often neglected, is the fact that only through the means of Outdoor Education can much of the content now included in science, social science, and the humanities become part of the reality of the student. This process establishes in the student a knowledge of an outdoor environment which was common in time and often personally well-known to those who have established today's curricula and who have written textbooks used by today's students.[6]

He further pointed out that urban communities have divorced themselves further and further from the natural world. The country background and past experiences with the natural environment that many of today's teachers have had makes them assume that their

[6] Brown, "The Academic Aspect of Outdoor Education," *Extending Education*, VI, No. 1, September 1961.

students understand their "language," when in reality much of this language is meaningless to the urbanized student. Brown also indicated that as a result of new developments personal knowledge gained from past rural experiences may no longer be of value.

Learning experiences in the outdoors have certain advantages over learning gained in the classroom. Dean Brown pointed this out when he wrote:

> The medium of Outdoor Education tends to reduce the all too prevalent verbalism in our classes. It gives a meaning to content and thereby makes subject matter more interesting, manageable, challenging, and applicable for many members of the class. Greater retention of usable knowledge should result from personal experience in the field.

The author then presents a dramatic personal experience to support his statement.

> Standing for the first time, high on the Columbia ice field in the shadow of a huge hanging glacier straining itself over the lip of a cirque, a teacher with 20 years of experience once said:
>
> "I've read about ice; I've talked about ice; I've taught about the ice age, and Norway and Switzerland—but now for the first time, I know what ice is!"

William H. Kilpatrick, the well-known educator and a proponent of the activity method of instruction seems to support the values inherent in direct-learning experiences when he states that people learn only those things which they live.

Outdoor education would not have significant relevance to school curriculum objectives were it not for the direct, practical, and meaningful experiences associated with it and academic subjects. The question, nevertheless, remains, "Do outdoor education experiences, whereby subject matter learned in the classroom is practically applied and supplemented in the outdoor environment, contribute more effectively to the achievement of elementary, junior high, and high school educational objectives?" The authors of this book believe so, based on the material gathered for this book and from personal experiences in the field.

Some educators may argue that since the effectiveness of outdoor education seems to be primarily dependent upon the use of the activity method, why not simply dispense with the outdoors as a classroom and employ greater use of the activity method in the formal classroom? The answer is that there are experiences which simply cannot be duplicated in the classroom. How, for instance, can a child truly comprehend what a mile is when he is told it is 5,280 feet or what an acre is when informed it contains 43,560 square feet? One must walk a mile and one must walk over, or at least look at, an acre of land before he can truly know what these measurements represent. No visual aid or other teaching method could ever duplicate the thrill a child receives when he spots a deer for the first time in the wild; nor could a classroom visual aid method ever duplicate the feeling received when, after a discussion on how mountains are formed, actually standing at the base of an extinct volcano or at the base of a mountain formed by some other geologic process. Also to be considered are the values gained from the living together experiences shared by the students and their teachers.

Outdoor Education and the Activity Method

Outdoor education, as it is related to the school curriculum, employs the activity and project method of instruction which is thought by many educators to be superior to the traditional recitation method. The activity method gives students opportunities to work on meaningful projects which dovetail with their current interests. In a study conducted by a number of New York City schools in which the traditional method of teaching and the activity method were compared, the following conclusions were noted:

1. In the schools which employed the activity method the students learned formal subjects almost as well as those learning by the traditional method while spending less time on them. In the actual use of skills, the activity students did as well as the traditional students. In the Comprehensive Test, which determined accomplishment in a much broader sense (general and practical knowledge of the world) the activity students were consistently superior.[7] In a further study of the same program made by Jersild it was shown that the activity students were better skilled in: drawing basic and sound conclusions from graphs and sound arguments, locating information, knowledge of current news, and application of generalizations to new problems in social studies and science.

---

[7] Saul B. Sells, John J. Loftus, and Louis Herbert, "Evaluative Studies of the Activity Program in the New York City Public Schools: A Preliminary Report," *Journal of Experimental Education,* IX (1941), pp. 310–322.

2. The activity students manifested more ability and interest in verbal discussions, arts and crafts, initiative, and leadership.[8]
3. Additional outcomes of the activity method appear to be that children learn to accept responsibilities and learn how to work with others.

It appears that the activity method offers advantages over traditional methods which extend far beyond the formal learning of subject matter. It seems logical to assume that one cannot totally grasp certain subject matter unless there is an opportunity to apply it in real life situations. One cannot learn how to drive a car merely by reading a book about the fundamentals involved. Practical application of the knowledge gained is essential.

An experiment similar to the one performed with elementary schools was carried out on the high school level. The purpose of the study was to determine if departure from the traditional method of studying subjects as well as departure from traditional subjects would adversely affect a student's ability to do college work. Some thirty high schools and thirty-eight colleges cooperated in this nationally planned program. The colleges agreed to accept graduates from the experimental schools, regardless of the subjects they had studied, provided they were recommended by the principal. The experimental schools made many changes in courses. Current Social Problems, for example, was substituted in some schools for United States History.

Approximately one and a half thousand high school graduates from the experimental schools were involved. They were studied in comparison to students of similar ability who were products of traditional high school programs. Both groups had similar grade averages in college. Those from the experimental schools showed greater ability in subjects except for foreign language. In addition to surpassing the more traditional group in general intellectual abilities, such as resourcefulness, and intellectual curiosity, the experimental students were more involved in extracurricular activities, manifested more social awareness, and showed greater interest in the arts. In light of the above experiments then, it appears that schools can broaden the educational background and contribute substantially more to the educational development of their students

---

[8] Arthur T. Jersild and others, "A Further Comparison of Pupils in 'Activity' and 'Non-Activity' Schools," *Journal of Experimental Education,* IX (1941), pp. 303–309.

in innumerable ways, yet not hamper their skill in learning formal subjects.[9]

In further support of the educational value of the activity approach for development of the "whole" child is the observation made by Smith, Stanley, and Shores that "maturation and experience derived from everyday activities are as influential at this age (sixth grade), if not more so, than formal instruction in history and chronology."[10]

The Outdoors as a Laboratory

Learning through direct experience is certainly not new, at least not on the high school level. Science has long been taught in conjunction with laboratory work. But why should laboratory work be limited only to the pure sciences? The outdoors offers a vast laboratory with materials far beyond that which can be offered in an artificial indoor laboratory, for it provides teaching material not only in the pure sciences but in mathematics, history, language arts, social awareness, and much more. This comparatively new resource, the outdoor laboratory, has been recognized by many schools, universities, educational organizations, and by a number of states that have provided legal, financial, and public support to outdoor education. The names of specific schools, universities, and state agencies are referred to in other sections of this book.

Educating the Whole Child

Education has placed greater emphasis on educating the whole child. Many educators have recognized the school's responsibility to teach and to provide experiences in areas aside from the academic subjects. Development of the whole individual through learning to live together with others of varying socioeconomic backgrounds, for example, is also a responsibility of the schools.

Sharp made reference to this when he advocated that, "The school camp should be an integral part of the school plan. It is just as necessary as any one of the laboratories, or the shop, or the

---

[9] Dean and Enid Chamberlin, N. E. Drought, and W. E. Scott, *Did They Succeed in College?* (New York: Harper and Row, Publishers, 1942).

[10] Smith, Stanley, and Shores, *Fundamentals of Curriculum Development* (Yonkers On Hudson, N.Y.: World Book Co., 1950), p. 323.

library. The need to teach young people to live, work, and explore together is now recognized as an essential part of education."[11]

James A. Wylie supported the view that the classroom alone cannot educate the whole child when he wrote: "We live in an age where camping is not only needed but offers some opportunities in education and character building which cannot be obtained elsewhere."[12] School camping, as a supplement to the school curriculum, provides effective learning through living experiences. Wrightstone supported this principle when he said, "Education experiences should take place where they can be normal: frequently this is not in the school."[13] Thurston pointed out the social and educational values of a school camp experience: "In many instances there is a permanent improvement in student-teacher relationships, in attitudes of students, and in the quality of the school experiences following the camping program."[14] If education has begun the task of concentrating on the development of the whole child then it appears that camping has a rightful place in the total education program, for, as Sharp states, "Camp is a locale wherein real learning about living together, about nature, and about spiritual values of the 'great outdoors' takes place."[15]

Experimentation in School Camping

Studies of the literature and research reports reveal that school camp directors throughout the country are experimenting through trial and error, in their selection of the outdoor education experiences they provide students. Such experiences differ greatly among the schools.

A pilot school camping project was undertaken by the San Diego, California school system. There were three types of educational

---

[11] L. B. Sharp, "Camping and Outdoor Education," *National Education Association Journal,* May 1947, pp. 366–367.

[12] James A. Wylie, "Camping and Outdoor Schools," *Education,* LXXIII, No. 1, September 1952, p. 4.

[13] Jacob W. Wrightstone, *Appraisals of New Elementary School Practices* (New York: Bureau of Publications, Teachers College, Columbia University, 1938), p. 133.

[14] Lee M. Thurston, *Community School Camp* (Lansing, Mich.: Department of Public Instruction, 1950), pp. 31–32.

[15] *Extending Education Through Camping* (New York: Life Camps, Inc. 1948), p. 100.

contributions noted as a result of teacher, parent, and student evaluations of the experience. The contributions noted were:

1. More knowledge gained about the natural world, a better awareness of principles of health, and the development of more cooperativeness and self-confidence.
2. Development of new interests, new self-realizations, and spiritual gains.
3. Better understanding by the teacher of the students and better relationships between teachers and students.[16]

Further justification, however, must still be found for substituting outdoor education programs, such as a school camp experience, for normal classroom time. Answers must be given to the question, "Are there experiences which offer not only effective but unique contributions to the attainment of educational objectives, learning situations which are not and cannot be included in the formal classroom?" The remainder of this chapter will concern itself with this question.

Integrating Outdoor Education and the School Curriculum

Kleindienst in her study of school camp programs attempted to show how school camping experiences could and are being integrated with the school curriculum. The following principles developed by her may serve as a basis for organization of school camp programs at the sixth grade level in conjunction with the school curriculum and the needs of children.[17]

1. The school camp program should be organized primarily as an integral part of the total school program contributing to educational objectives and offering those experiences most effectively taught and learned in the out-of-doors.
2. The program should be based upon nature, needs, and interests of the participants and should be organized around problems and processes within their experience.
3. The school camp program should integrate all of its activities around problems inherent in group living out-of-doors and base its methodology upon fun, discovery, adventure, direct experiences, and active participation.
4. Experiences should be so organized as to give children an under-

---

[16] James Mitchell Clarke, *Public School Camping* (Stanford, California: Stanford University Press, 1951), p. 119.
[17] Kleindienst, *School Camp Programs*, p. 127.

standing of the problems, realities, and processes of social co-operation that result in more socialized human beings.

Kleindienst also developed the following principles to guide teachers in the selection of school camp program experiences for sixth grade children.

1. Those experiences should be selected and guided that make possible the achievement of success, satisfaction, and fun by the camper.
2. Experiences should be selected and guided with consideration given to maturity, development, skill, and experimental background of the campers as well as their needs, interests, and individuality.
3. Those experiences should be selected and guided that are vital and meaningful in the out-of-doors camping situation and through which skills can be taught and mastered with the greatest economy of time and general effectiveness.
4. Those experiences should be selected that expand the number of new and increase the meaningfulness of the old, educationally positive experiences, aid in the development of new meanings, and enlarge the child's understanding of important concepts.[18]

Many educators believe that the sixth grade is the ideal grade level for school camp programs. A child's natural curiosity is still strong and he is generally emotionally old enough to adapt to a living-away-from-home situation without a great deal of emotional stress. The difficulties confronted by the departmentalization of the junior and senior high schools has been the major deterrent in the development of programs at that level. Still, an increasing number of secondary schools have managed to overcome the problem in various ways. Students may receive advance assignments from their teachers in courses they will be missing and devote a part of each school camp day to completing their assignments.

The use of the outdoors provides countless opportunities for enriching and complementing school curricula at the elementary and secondary levels. Many of the activities listed on the following pages were obtained from printed material provided by schools throughout the country that conduct outdoor education programs.

Social Studies. The field of social studies involves man's understanding of his physical and social environment. It includes knowledge about the institutions which are essential to survival and the

[18] Kleindienst, *School Camp Programs,* pp. 130–132.

activities which contribute to man's effective operation as a member of society.

There are many excellent and practical examples of how outdoor education might contribute to the field of social studies. For example, a study might be made of the types of outdoor park and recreational facilities available in the local community. How were they obtained and developed? Who do they serve? What are the values inherent in these facilities?

A study involving the attitude of people toward the preservation of open space and natural areas for education and recreation might prove significant to the foregoing study. The study of the conservation movement in the United States and the politics involved in it, the natural resources of the country, and its economic and political effect upon the growth of the United States, should prove to be interesting to students.

Our country depends upon its natural resources, yet many of our resources are not being used wisely. More and more lakes, rivers, and streams are becoming polluted, as is the very air we breathe; natural scenic areas and land for outdoor recreation are becoming scarcer and scarcer. Surely the schools have a responsibility to teach the voting public of tomorrow an appreciation of, and the value of, our natural resources and how they may help to protect them. Outdoor education provides many conservation education experiences aimed at instilling in our young people . . . the citizens of tomorrow . . . new attitudes toward our natural heritage.

Field trips have been taken by classes in various schools to the sites of early industries developed in the local community; to abandoned farms to determine the factors which influenced the farmer to leave; to eroded hillsides and polluted bodies of water to foster discussions about conservation problems; to historical sites and areas; to local industries, such as a lumber mill, tree farm, milk plant, mine, dairy farm, and truck farm. All of these have helped reveal to students the changing patterns of a community.

At a resident school camp discussions have centered around group living problems. Students participate in a community camp government, and engage in group planning of various activities, such as cooking out and cleaning sleeping quarters. All these activities aid in development of the students' social awareness and responsibility to self and to the total group.

Other activities related to social studies include:

- Learning about local customs;
- Studying the history of the past Indian tribes of the area;
- Organizing and participating in an Indian ceremonial typical of the local tribe;
- Constructing early pioneer tools out of natural materials and using them to dramatize the life of the pioneer;
- Learning the effects of local natural resources upon the cultural life and traditions of the early pioneer;
- Studying the economic, recreational, and aesthetic values of the local natural resources;
- Studying the problems of land use and migrating populations;
- Conducting conservation projects in camp and in the local community;
- Learning campcraft and woodlore skills which aid in living comfortably in the outdoors;
- Making maps and reading them;
- Developing cooperative solutions to problems;
- Carrying out democratic living in a camp;
- Developing and improving interpersonal relationships.

Science. Never before in the history of education has so much attention been given to the sciences. The many scientific breakthroughs in space, atomic energy, and medicine make it essential that students understand what is happening in the field of science.

Science taught only within the confines of the classroom is devoid of a great deal of realism and meaning. A thousand models or pictures will never replace the learning experiences which occur when a student, under guidance of a skilled teacher, collects material for a terrarium, and then observes the biological principles of growth and survival taking place.

In the outdoors all of man's senses are utilized to their fullest. The outdoors offers real life science teaching situations for which there are no substitutes. Microclimates cannot be adequately duplicated in the classroom, nor can the principles and concepts involved in conservation of natural resources be completely understood while sitting at a desk and looking at a picture of an eroded field or a polluted stream.

The outdoors serves as a rich source of materials for the study of botany, zoology, entomology, ecology, paleontology, geology, herpetology, meteorology and astronomy.

Following is a list of typical science activities which are included in outdoor education programs:

Studying the physical features of the local terrain—how it was formed, composition of local rocks and minerals and how they were formed;
Breaking apart, analyzing, and identifying rocks and minerals;
Observing evidence of the interdependence of all living and inanimate things;
Studying behavior of animal life through observation of animal tracks and other evidences indicating their activity;
Using microscope and hand lens while making field studies of minute pond life, soil, and other elements of nature;
Observing biological principles including predation, survival, parasitism, symbiosis, photosynthesis, competition, dominance, plant succession, biotic communities, and transmission of seeds;
Becoming more familiar with the value of the wildlife, vegetation, soil, rocks, and minerals of the area;
Deducing through evidence why certain forms of animal life and plant life live in a particular area and not elsewhere;
Learning principles involved in predicting the weather and maintaining a weather station;
Learning certain biological principles found within a terrarium and aquarium;
Studying construction habits of birds (nests), spiders (webs), insects (cocoons);
Making soil experiments (testing and classifying);
Using simple keys for identification of insects and plants;
Testing water for drinking purposes;
Studying different types of vegetation at different elevations;
Studying astronomy through use of a telescope;
Learning the principles of leverage in moving boulders and logs;
Interpreting topographic maps;
Observing how soil erosion and forest fires affect the ecology of a given area;
Learning forest and wildlife management practices;
Learning elementary techniques of taxidermy;
Developing skill in the proper use of a compass;
Correcting and preventing, through work projects, soil erosion;
Planting and maintaining a garden;
Learning principles of plant grafting and crossbreeding of plants.

Language Arts. The language arts include all the communication skills of reading, writing, speaking, listening, and thinking. They utilize both the graphic and dramatic arts to foster understanding.

It is difficult to read much prose and poetry without finding reference to the beauties of the natural world. Thoreau, Hemingway, Wordsworth, and Longfellow are only a few writers who dealt extensively with nature in their writings. The informal atmosphere inherent in outdoor education programs offers many opportunities for creative expression by students. Indeed, what more natural and ideal place is there for writing a poem or story about the outdoors than *in* the outdoors?

There are many activities in outdoor education which aid the development of communications skills in students. They include:

Making field notes;
Writing letters home or to conservation agencies for information;
Writing reports about camp activities;
Maintaining a daily log;
Writing stories about the outdoors;
Utilizing camp library for reference material and literature concerned with the outdoors;
Writing reports and evaluations of field trips and other activities;
Reading Indian stories;
Storytelling;
Writing and acting in plays related to the history of the local area;
Writing reports and articles for the camp newspaper;
Locating documented evidence of observations and deductions made in the field;
Labeling specimens and nature trails;
Preparing and presenting a school assembly program about camp experiences;
Reading and listening to stories, prose, and poetry about the outdoors while seated around a campfire;
Taking an active part in discussions involved in planning and evaluating trips;
Making oral reports about field trips.

Mathematics. Along with science, mathematics has taken on new significance in modern technology. Yet, the analogue computor with its tremendous capacity for work still is dependent upon the human brain for its direction and instruction.

Mathematics becomes more significant and meaningful to the student when he discovers practical applications for the mathematical knowledge he has gained. Outdoor education programs provide countless opportunities for such applications. In addition, a student is more apt to understand certain mathematical concepts when these concepts are transferred into real situations.

Following is a listing of activities conducted in the outdoors which help to make the study of mathematics more meaningful:

- Taking measurements of a tree involving board feet;
- Learning and using a forester's formula for measuring the yield of lumber from a given tree;
- Determining the size of certain areas through the use of such measurements as acres, square miles, square yards, and square feet;
- Determining the flow of a given stream per second (cubic measurements);
- Determining the cubic yards of dirt necessary to fill in an eroded area;
- Learning how to use map instruments;
- Surveying; making maps or scale models of the local terrain;
- Making graphs of daily weather records;
- Pacing the distance during a hike; determining time required to walk a mile;
- Estimating the percentage of areas containing swamps, fields, and woodlands;
- Determining the percent of a slope;
- Determining the time of day through the use of a sun dial;
- Determining the distance across a lake and the height of a tree or a mountain through the use of geometric principles;
- Reading weather instruments, and calculating temperature averages and barometric readings;
- Learning the use of a compass (orienteering);
- Determining amounts and computing the cost of food consumed in camp or for a special cookout, and the cost per person per meal;
- Operating a banking system at camp and a camp store, and keeping records of all operations;
- Demonstrating the practical application of mathematics in the construction of a bridge or a retaining pool;
- Drawing plans for a bird house;
- Demonstrating the laws of leverage through lifting logs and moving boulders;
- Computing the obvious and hidden financial costs of a school camp trip;
- Observing geometric patterns in nature.

Art and Music. The outdoors abounds in a variety of subjects for photography, sketching, modeling, painting, and contains many natural materials which help to encourage creativity in students through arts and crafts. Engaging in art activities in the outdoors helps to develop in students powers of observation and an appreciation of the beauty found in the natural world. Music, too, has its place in the outdoors, for it was here that music was born—through crude musical instruments made from objects in nature. There are numerous examples in the outdoors to demonstrate the first musical instruments made from natural materials by the American Indian.

Here are examples of art and music activities which are often contained in outdoor education programs:

Using natural materials as designs for various works of art;
Designing bird houses;
Making ceramic or wood models of animals;
Collecting and arranging dried bouquets of flowers;
Drawing and painting local outdoor scenes;
Preparing nature trail signs, charts and other illustrations of natural phenomena;
Collecting seeds, flowers, grasses, and stones for making special creative arrangements;
Listening to and recording bird calls and songs, frogs, insects, a running stream, wind in the trees;
Making leaf and fern prints through use of various media;
Constructing a relief map of the camp area;
Designing charts and exhibits of natural objects;
Learning and singing folk songs and studying their meaning;
Making Indian musical artifacts such as drums or rattles for special Indian programs;
Hiking in rhythm while singing camp songs;
Listening to the music of Beethoven (*Pastorale*), Edward McDowall (*Woodland Sketches*), Groffé (*Grand Canyon Suite*), and others and relating them to the outdoors.

Physical education, health, and recreation. The outdoors offers a variety of opportunities to learn skills in physical education and recreation, and in the practice of health and sanitation. Following is a description of such activities included in present outdoor education programs:

Health

Planning menus;
Developing proper eating habits;
Learning to dress properly for the outdoors, depending upon the season;
Learning precautions to follow when looking for drinking water outdoors;
Learning first aid.

Recreation

Square and folk dancing;
Participating in active games played by Indians and pioneers;
Participating in nature scavenger hunts;
Learning the techniques of hunting, fishing, boating, archery, fly tying and bait casting, skiing, orienteering, woodcraft, photography;
Developing hobbies related to natural history;

Snowshoeing and ice skating;
Swimming.

Physical Education

Hiking;
Cutting logs for firewood;
Learning the proper way to ascend and descend a steep slope;
Learning to use forest tools properly;
Building and extinguishing a campfire;
Planting trees;
Trailing and tracking;
Learning the techniques of survival.

Homemaking. Homemaking can be greatly enriched, and made more meaningful and interesting when carried on in an outdoor setting, for it is there where it had its beginning.

Homemaking activities found in outdoor education programs include:

Identifying, collecting, and cooking local edible plants;
Identifying and learning about the many uses of herbs, including use for medicinal and cooking purposes, and learning how to grow them;
Studying diet habits of wildlife;
Planning camp menus;
Planning, preparing and serving food at a cookout;
Conducting camp kitchen duties;
Studying the natural sources of dyes;
Using proper clothing in the outdoors;
Maintaining clean campgrounds and dining hall;
Practicing proper table manners during camp mealtimes.

It has been noted in this chapter that most units of study in the school's curriculum can be supplemented through the use of the outdoors. Indeed, there are some learning experiences, as already revealed, which cannot take place within the confines of classrooms.

Outdoor education is not a subject in itself. It is a unique learning medium for helping students to gain more meaning and better understanding of the subjects to which they are exposed. The old axiom that a picture is worth a thousand words suggests that a direct experience can be worth a thousand pictures.

CHAPTER IV

Resources for Outdoor Education

An outdoor interpretive program in natural history and conservation opens the gateway to a greater understanding and appreciation of natural phenomena through utilization of the outdoor environment—the soil, water, minerals, and animal and plant life in their natural habitat. It is unrealistic to expect students to gain a full understanding of their natural environment without the tools found in the outdoors.

It is the purpose of this chapter to identify the many potential resources for outdoor education found in and around the local community.

Nature Is Everywhere

Physical resources for conducting outdoor education programs are, despite the rapid disappearance of open space in our cities, still available in every city, town, or village in the country. Some communities are more fortunate than others in that they have large tracts of open land areas, usually in the form of parks or private estates, available for their use. Other communities have state parks situated near them, or even a national park or fish hatchery, while still others have none of the foregoing facilities. Yet, there is not a community in America, including our major cities, that does not have a piece of soil, indigenous vegetation, even if only "weeds," insects, birds, mammals, amphibians, reptiles, fish, geologic features, running streams, and examples of soil erosion. Finally, no matter where one is, the weather is always available for study. What is needed, however, is a willingness to learn, enthusiasm, an observing eye, and a gift of imagination. Carlson had this observation to make about a vacant city lot and its potential for the study of natural phenomena:

> I have for over two years watched a neglected fifty foot lot in a metropolitan area. Here I have observed 28 species of birds, including one ring-necked pheasant; 5 trees, 8 shrubs, and herbaceous plants, not all yet identified, running into the scores. Two snakes,

> mice, cottontail rabbits, and hundreds of species of insects have been seen there. Through a magnifying glass, I have watched the young aphids being born alive, and the pupae of the lady-bird beetles feeding on the aphids. The drama of life goes on in intensity even in this unsightly, weed filled "vacant" lot.[1]

John Kieran in his book "A Natural History of New York" points out that even in New York City wildlife and other natural things exist almost everywhere if one would only make the effort to look.[2]

Another excellent description of the abundance of natural objects found in almost every city in the United States is the Audubon Nature Bulletin written by Dorothy A. Treat.[3]

Quality Versus Quantity

There are some teachers who are reluctant to conduct programs in the outdoors unless there are large tracts of natural areas available in which to roam around. There is also a tendency for some outdoor education leaders during a field trip to pay more attention to covering distance than to walking slowly, stopping often to observe and to investigate. One can gain basically the same understanding of the concepts and principles of the natural world on an acre of land as on a hundred or even a thousand acres. A class and its teacher staked out a square yard of earth and found over 15 species of plants and about the same number of insects.

It is the *quality* of teaching that is involved and not the quantity. This, of course, is not to say that the teacher who has twenty-five acres at his disposal is no better off than the teacher who only has an acre of land to walk upon and study. No matter how vivid a person's imagination is, he receives a much different feeling when viewing, in real life, a badly eroded farm for the first time, as he does when looking at a leader's classroom demonstration of the same process. Nothing can take the place of the awe and humbleness one feels when walking among the giant Sequoias in the Redwood Forest of California. Nevertheless, it remains true that one

---

[1] Reynold E. Carlson, "Enriching the School Curriculum," *The Bulletin of the National Association of Secondary School Principals,* May 1947, p. 127.

[2] John Kieran, *A Natural History of New York* (New York: Houghton Mifflin Company, 1959).

[3] Dorothy A. Treat, "City Nature," *Audubon Nature Bulletin* (New York: National Audubon Society, 1955).

can still learn much about the natural world in a comparatively small area. For example, a skilled teacher can utilize a tree on the school's own property as a teaching object, and literally cover the world of microorganisms, higher forms of plants and animals, geology, conservation, and the entire universe for that matter.

The teacher may first, through the question technique (wording her questions in such a way that the student, although not knowledgeable in a particular area, will, through logical deduction, arrive at the correct answer), inform students of the specific usefulness of the tree to man.

The redwood, for example, is used for siding on houses because of its beauty and natural resistance to the elements. The teacher's next step may be to encourage students to identify the tree by instructing them how to use a tree key, including the scientific terminology for identifying the various characteristics of the physical structure of plants.

Once the tree has been identified, the teacher may, through questions, help students discover the general usefulness of the tree to other forms of life around it. Perhaps it serves as a support for a bird's nest. "Will all species of birds nest in this tree?" "No." At this point the teacher may lead the students into a discussion on bird behavior. The tree may also harbor insects. Perhaps some can be found in the tree, precipitating a discussion about insects in general, and the various plant diseases which they help spread. This may lead further into a discussion of fungus and bacteria.

While the students are gathered under the tree, they are certain to notice the difference in temperature if it is a warm, sunny day. This can be the beginning of the study of weather and the influence which plants have upon the weather through the phenomena of transpiration. "What happens to a tree when it dies?" "It reverts back to the soil with the aid of chemical weathering (another starting point for a discussion of weather), insects, and fungus." "What are the ingredients which make up soil?" Thus, a study of soil enters the picture. Trees also hold soil intact. "What would happen if the tree was cut down?" The concepts of soil erosion and conservation make their introduction. "Notice that the roots of the tree are making the cement sidewalk rise." "Plants in general help in the process of breaking up rocks." "What are rocks made of?" "Notice that most of the branches of this tree have a tendency to grow in one general direction. The side of the tree closest to the building has relatively few branches (principles involved in the growth of trees). Why?" Students become engaged in the subject of the sun and photosynthesis. The sun itself, and its influence upon all life and upon nonliving things, may be the starting point for a discussion of the heavens.

With this start the teacher may lead his class away from the tree to observe some of the other elements which might have entered the discussion. Examples of soil erosion may be close by. A home with a garden in front of it may be across the street. There, soil from the garden might be observed which has collected on the sidewalk after the rain of the previous night. Students might see that the soil came from a bare spot in the garden where there was insufficient grass or other vegetation to hold it back. Thus, the teacher brings the class into a discussion of soil erosion. Such learning situations are plentiful in every community; a lawn in front of the school building, a sidewalk where small plants thrive between the cracks, or an empty lot. The resources for outdoor education are virtually unlimited.

School Sites

A large number of newly constructed schools have had—and lost—a priceless facility for teaching natural science and conservation. Since most elementary and high schools are not oriented toward using the school site for educational purposes the land around the school too often is cleared of trees, running brooks are filled in, and the natural area which might well have served as an effective outdoor laboratory gives way to asphalt playgrounds and manicured lawns. Communities actually spend money destroying these valuable natural areas! On the other hand, some communities are fortunate to have school officials, teachers, and local citizens who would not permit this to happen. As a result they have left much of their undeveloped land intact for educational purposes. Alert teachers in many of these schools have found innumerable ways of incorporating these natural areas into their curriculums.

Such areas, which contain the flora and fauna indigenous to the local scene, are, in essence, outdoor laboratories where students may obtain direct contact with their natural world. It is here that explorations can be engaged in to cover such subjects as ecology, botany, ornithology, entomology, herpetology, geology, meteorology, marine biology, and other fields of science.

It is not necessary to have the entire outdoor laboratory on the school site. Larger sites are needed. They may be located elsewhere in the community, such as in community parks, and maintained by students from the schools.

There is a great need for more schools to acquire more land and to plan for outdoor education programs, for it is the young people of today who will be in a position to decide the fate of much of the nation's natural outdoor areas tomorrow. Students need to be informed of the value of open space for their recreational, economic, esthetic, and educational values. What better place is there than on school property to develop in our youth an appreciation and respect for our natural heritage? Galbreath pointed out the need and importance of "outdoor laboratories" for schools when he wrote:

> Due to the elimination of natural areas by ever-expanding superhighways, suburbia, and industry, there is developing a greater need, in every school and especially in the big high school, for an outdoor laboratory, readily accessible the year round, and dedicated permanently to the study of outdoor biology, where the wise use of natural resources may be studied first hand through scientific and educational investigation.[4]

A number of schools throughout the country have acquired property large enough to accommodate not only the school building and facilities for physical education but outdoor education programs as well. One good example is the Edgemont School in Scarsdale, New York which has a seventy acre site where twenty acres have been set aside for outdoor education purposes.

A school's own property is a good place to initiate outdoor education programs. For one thing, it is convenient for classes to participate in outdoor activities right on the school property. More frequent excursions can be made on the property during class time. On the other hand a facility located some distance from the school would involve more time and probably mean adjustment of the class schedule. Another factor to be considered is that the students generally seem to take more interest and pride in an area located on their school property than in that which does not belong to the school.

When a community plans to purchase property for a new school, or when an established school is planning to acquire more property,

---

[4] J. W. Galbreath, "The Value of a Nature Area in Teaching Biology and Conservation," *Illinois Educational Press Bulletin,* March 1960, p. 20.

the following check list may serve to determine the suitability of the land for outdoor education purposes:

1. Does at least part of the property offer a variety of geologic features, such as uneven terrain and rock out-croppings?
2. Does a stream or other body of water run through the property or is one close by?
3. Is there a variety of vegetation indigenous to the local area?
4. Is there a sufficient variety of wildlife?

The more there is of the above the more the outdoor education program may be enriched.

5. Can the property be protected by a sufficient buffer zone to protect it against present or future adjacent housing or similar developments?

If the school board is considering whether to add ten acres or twenty-five acres of land to its school site for outdoor education it should choose the larger acreage. A larger site will permit greater variety of activities, and will enable the school to establish permanent outdoor stations. In any event, a minimum of ten acres of land is suggested for an outdoor education program.

Schools limited in the availability of outdoor space often bring elements of the outdoors into the school building. Caution must be practiced here, however, for there is a tendency on the part of some teachers to want to bring in too much of the outdoors. Students bring in insects, frogs, salamanders, plants, snakes, cocoons—and whatever else they might discover around their homes or on trips. These students could be stimulated to develop terrariums, aquariums, and construct dioramas out of the natural objects they bring to class.

Forests

A significant number of schools throughout the country have developed educational programs in connection with forests, either on school property or on community or state property. These areas have become known as school forests. (See Chapter II.) They serve as excellent outdoor education classrooms. Programs in forestry involving public school children are found in more than half of the states in this country.

Forests offer an unlimited variety of educational resource material for teachers and students. Following are just a few of the many activities which might be conducted in a forest environment:

1. Thinning and pruning trees (forest management practices).
2. Harvesting and selling Christmas trees to the local community. (This has already become a tradition in some communities.)
3. Preparation of maps.
4. Study of the interrelationships and interdependencies of plants and animals in a forest environment.
5. Fish and stream management.
6. Effect of a forest environment on the local weather.
7. Wildlife and vegetation census.
8. Study of geologic features.
9. Study of soil erosion and practice of corrective measures.
10. Study of plant succession and forest climax.

State parks and forests are excellent resources for conducting outdoor education programs. Unfortunately, however, few communities are close enough to one to take advantage of them. Yet, many states are anxious to have their parks and forests used for outdoor education programs so that, among other reasons, people will become more educated as to the recreational and economic value of such areas and learn to appreciate and respect them. Some states conduct special outdoor education programs in their parks and forests or permit outside groups to use their facilities extensively. Michigan has developed camp facilities for use by school districts throughout the state.

As is true with state parks and forests, there are relatively few communities which are close enough to take advantage of national reserves. The National Parks System has an extensive educational program for visitors—individuals and groups alike. Many national parks maintain trailside museums, nature trails, and full-time naturalists, who conduct field trips, lectures, and slide programs. The national parks have been established, as a general rule, in areas which are unique in some way. The uniqueness may have to do with an historic event or with a natural physical feature.

Farms

It has been predicted that by the year 2000, fewer than ten percent of the population will be producing the food requirements of the nation. The balance of the people will be the consumers. Thus, future generations can be expected to have little, if any, direct contact with the soil. How may future generations acquire a real understanding of the world's problems of growing food and timber without firsthand experiences?

There are many children who have never seen live farm animals. Indeed some of these children, more than likely, scarcely know such animals exist. They have only seen milk in containers and bottles and eggs in paper cartons purchased at the supermarket. Modern civilization is still dependent upon the agricultural farm for much of its food; consequently, children should be made aware of its importance in their daily lives.

While it is true that class field trips have been made to farms by schools for years, the idea of a school-owned farm is a relatively new development in the field of education. (See Chapter II, page 25.) Most states have high schools which either own or rent a farm. Schools do not have to own farms. It is possible for schools to locate a farmer who would be willing to cooperate with the local school district by making his farm available to outdoor education classes. A farm may not only serve as an outdoor laboratory for the study of agriculture, for if the land is typical of the area, encompassing a variety of natural features such as a running stream, pond, and woodlot, the farm may well serve as the center for much of the school's outdoor education program.

The potential program activities available at the average farm include:

1. Observing and caring for domestic farm animals, including milking cows, feeding chickens, collecting eggs, and other general farm chores.
2. Tapping maple trees and making maple syrup.
3. Learning the purpose of, and how to use and maintain various farm machinery (learning physical science principles and concepts in the process).
4. Planting and caring for a vegetable and herb garden.
5. Conservation activities such as: contour plowing, strip cropping, terracing, planting vegetation to serve as food and cover for wildlife, and pond management.
6. Hunting, fishing, and other outdoor sports.
7. Study of indigenous vegetation and wildlife and geologic features.

Experimental farms are often operated by university departments of agriculture or by the federal government. One finds on such farms the latest conservation and animal husbandry techniques, as well as experimental plantings of disease resistant plants, experiments involving biological control of insects, the use of new insecticide and planticide sprays.

Camps

Many school systems throughout the country purchase or lease children's camps located outside of the school district, sometimes as far away as 100 miles. The camps must be winterized if they are to be utilized during the colder months. There are a number of summer camp directors who have winterized their camps and rent them to school districts for school camping purposes during the fall, winter, and spring. Many colleges and universities, which very early recognized the value of a resident school camping experience, have developed their own outdoor education centers with a resident school camp, and have made them available to schools at a relatively low cost. Most of the colleges and universities also help provide the schools with skilled leaders who are outdoor education specialists.

Summer camps offer wonderful opportunities for the development of outdoor education programs. Many of them contain a wealth of natural resources on their property. Unfortunately, most summer camps fail to take advantage of these opportunities. The study of natural history all too often plays a minor role in the camp's program.

On the other hand, there are some camp directors who would like to include outdoor education activities in their programs but are unable to secure adequate leadership. This obstacle has been partially overcome by camps by offering a counselor, who has an interest in nature education, a scholarship to attend one of the many outdoor education workshops held throughout the country, or a scholarship to attend a National Audubon Camp. The Audubon Camps offer programs to counselors, teachers, and others who are interested in acquiring outdoor education leadership skills.

Zoological Parks

The zoo has been the object of class field trips for many years, although it has never reached its full potential. So much more can be learned by children at the zoo other than merely reading the labels which identify the various species found there. A skillful teacher can turn the classic zoo visit into a very effective teaching tool by preparing in advance of the visit a series of questions related to the science unit she may be teaching. Such questions encourage the children to make keener observations than they might otherwise do.

Some zoos have expanded their facilities to include printed materials on animals from around the world, demonstration programs, development of various types of zoology clubs including bird study and study of amphibians and reptiles. Other zoos, realizing that not everyone can visit their facilities, or in order to make their zoo better known, will bring a representative sample of it as a traveling zoo to the surrounding communities. The program is usually conducted during the summer months and involves bringing both wild and domestic animals to playgrounds and parks with a skilled naturalist who lectures and conducts demonstrations.

Parks

Many city parks offer little in the way of natural areas, that is, natural features unaltered by man. Nevertheless, much can still be learned about the phenomena of nature in a traditional park. The well-trimmed lawns and exotic species of trees and shrubs harbor much insect life. Principles of tree growth and photosynthesis can be observed and studied even if the trees are exotic species. Some soil erosion is found even in the best-kept parks. Geologic features will undoubtedly be available for study. Certainly, there will be native birds for observation and study. Native species of amphibians and fish will most likely be found in and near ponds.

Regardless of the type of plant life found in city parks, very noticeable changes take place in the vegetation at different seasons of the year in most sections of the country. In addition, changes can also be noted in the animal life. Certain animals hibernate during the winter in areas of the country where there are extremes of temperatures, some birds and insects migrate, and drastic changes can be observed in the life cycle of moths, butterflies, and other insects. Thus, school classes can return to the same park several times during the year, observe, and learn something new upon each visit.

What more appropriate place is there than in a park to read the writings of Walt Whitman and other poets who have written about nature while sitting on the grass under a shaded tree, or what better place is there to sketch or paint the natural world?

A good deal about conservation can be learned, and proper conservation attitudes can be developed by students in the well-kept city park, particularly if it is a small park serving a rather large area. A number of city parks, for instance, maintain wildlife sanctuaries. City park directors are constantly on guard to prevent destruction of their parks' flora and fauna by the many people who visit. This concern can be transferred by the teacher to the monumental problems of utilizing properly all of our country's natural resources, the legislation enacted, and the legislation and education still needed to protect these resources from being over-used and from wilful destruction.

Many city parks have historical importance, making them ideal as a supplementary aid in the teaching of history. There are many park managers who are now beginning to realize the potential educational value of their parks and who are also aware that if they are to be appreciated, respected, and used intelligently by the general public, people need to be educated about them. As a result, parks are hiring naturalists, building nature trails, providing written materials on various aspects of nature, emphasizing what might be found in a particular park, providing lecturers to visit schools, and helping teachers who come to the parks with their classes in whatever way they can.

A fine resource guide to help elementary school teachers use city parks for the enrichment of their science curriculums was developed by Weiss. Although the guide was primarily designed for use by teachers in the New York City area, much of the material can apply equally well to almost any city park in the country. It covers concepts, aims and objectives, suggested activities, possible outcomes of a trip to a park, and has a bibliography for teachers and one for students on books, films, recordings, and written material.[5]

Park-School

The development of leisure-time skills is being recognized by many educators as a school responsibility which should be integrated into the regular curriculum. As a result, a greater number of schools are taking advantage of the potential outdoor education possibilities which local community parks can offer for recreational and educational purposes.

---

[5] Irving J. Weiss, "Enriching Science Through Outdoor Education," A Resource Guide for Teaching the Use of the Park in the Elementary Schools (unpublished Doctoral thesis, New York University, 1961).

The park-school concept which has become a reality in a number of communities throughout the country, involves integrating a park, a school, certain types of recreational facilities, and a community into a single, unified, over-all program. A formal agreement between the city, which has jurisdiction over the park, and the school board is usually made. The park-school idea is more than simply putting a number of facilities together on a given site. It involves the cooperation of the city or town governments, the school system, and agencies concerned with the educational and recreational needs of both youth and adults.

The many obstacles which, in the past, prevented cooperation between city parks and school systems for the educational use of parks is being eliminated. Park directors have become more aware that the need for protection of parks will assume less importance, and the proper use of their parks will come about more rapidly, when the local community becomes better educated in the use of its natural resources. In addition, an educated and sympathetic community will usually react more favorably to the acquisition of more park land as population increases cause the need for more park facilities.

Botanical Gardens

Botanical gardens generally feature not only exotic plantings but plantings indigenous to the local area. They usually include shrubs, flowers and trees. Such gardens are also usually quite rich in birdlife because of the variety of habitats which meet the requirements of many species of birds. Insects, frogs, and toads also abound in botanical gardens. Some gardens offer special programs—classes for children as well as adults. The classes cover a wide variety of areas related to plants including care and propagation, grafting, insect control, plant identification, and raising of vegetables.

Nature Centers

Most nature centers primarily consist of an educational building or buildings, a full-time naturalist staff, and a natural area. They differ from the trailside museum in that the latter is usually situated on public land, owned and operated by state or federal government, and serves transient visitors. On the other hand the nature center is more of a community development primarily serving the local citizenry. The nature center, like the trailside museum, is concerned with the natural phenomena unique to the local area. It seeks to interpret local natural history for the community. Both the trailside museum and the nature center differ from a museum in that the former usually contain a natural outdoor area which serves as a laboratory; museums generally do not have such areas. The nature center and trailside museum aid in *use* of the outdoors whereas the museum places greater emphasis upon the display of objects.

The National Audubon Society, realizing the need for such centers, established a Nature Centers Division which encourages and assists communities, through technical and consulting services, in the establishment of nature and conservation centers.

In some communities, a number of prominent citizens have formed corporations, promoted the nature center concept and initiated a fund drive, acquired the necessary land for the program, constructed an outdoor education building, and operated the center. In other communities, the local government has assumed this responsibility.

The centers are open year-round with full time naturalist-directors and other staff members. Usually these centers are supported in part by the city government and by private contributions and memberships. They cater not only to children, but to adult interests, too, with programs for daily school visits to the centers, field trips, lectures, and workshops for teachers in natural history and conservation. If a school is fortunate enough to have its own natural area, the center staff is often willing to help the school make the best use of its own land.

Nature centers may contain such features as exhibits, a science laboratory and science library, live native animals, nature trails, model farm, weather station, garden plots, and trails for the physically handicapped. Some centers have even developed special nature trails for the blind. Nature center programs may include field trips, staff visitations to local schools to help classes plan outdoor education programs, materials for loan, lectures and demonstrations, educational films, special workshops, hobby clubs, science round-table discussions, courses and special activities for the physically handicapped and mentally retarded.

Museums

There was a time when all general museums of natural history found in cities merely collected, preserved, and exhibited specimens. Today, however, in many museums, the public is encouraged to participate while in the museum. Consequently, there are a number of museums, such as The Museum of Natural History in New York City, which now offers classes in various aspects of natural history, field trips, plus other programs for the benefit of the general public. Such museums have become activity centers and thus are helping to eliminate the passive role which all visitors once played.

Children's museums, although they often place much emphasis upon natural history, differ from nature centers in that the former do not usually have their own natural areas in which to conduct outdoor education programs. Junior museums are found throughout the country and are being promoted to a great extent by the Natural Science for Youth Foundation. Many of these museums conduct outdoor education programs including field trips, utilizing nearby or, in some cases, distant parks and natural areas. These museums are operated either privately by local community citizens, by parks and recreation agencies, or by school systems.

Trailside museums have been established on lands owned by colleges, universities, and national, state, and city parks. The trailside museum, unlike a general museum of natural history, concerns itself, as a rule, with an interpretation of local natural history. Often raising more questions than it answers, the trailside museum helps the viewer traverse the nature trails emanating from the museum. The museum through its various displays, including live animals indigenous to the local area, provides the viewer with detailed information of what he is apt to observe along the trail. It also attempts to get across certain biologic, geologic and/or other principles and concepts which may be difficult for the inexperienced trailer to pick up himself. School classes frequently visit such museums on a half or full day basis. The museums are usually staffed with naturalists who may lead field trips for a nominal sum or sometimes at no charge.

Fish Hatcheries

State fish hatcheries are excellent locations for a field trip. The personnel in fish hatcheries are usually pleased to conduct a class tour of the hatchery and explain its operation. Students learn about life cycles of fish and the specific requirements for propagation and survival. There is also an opportunity for students to observe closely live native species of fish, an opportunity not readily available when students are in the woods, unless, of course, one is fortunate enough to hook one on the end of a fishing line.

Nurseries

A nursery is an excellent place for students to learn about plant propagation and proper care of plants, and to observe the variety of exotic plants, and native and exotic trees. Proprietors of nurseries are often delighted to conduct a class on a tour of their greenhouses and grounds.

Reservoirs and Dams

A reservoir is an ideal place to take a field trip. It is usually surrounded by watersheds rich in natural resources. Permission is often needed to enter reservoir areas but a school class should not encounter any difficulty, provided an appointment is made in advance. A reservoir offers a treasure house of water life to study, and usually contains a considerable wooded area around the shore with a variety of plant and animal life. Students are introduced to the entire operation involved in supplying a city with clean, potable water for drinking and other purposes.

A flood control dam is a starting off point for a discussion on what causes floods, how they can be controlled, and prevented. River navigation and electric power are often other products of man-made dams.

Seashore

The coastline of the United States and shore line of lakes offer unlimited opportunities for the study of many forms of marine life.

The sea in particular provides a tremendous variety of both plant and animal life—from microscopic plants to giant seaweed and from hermit crabs to whales, the largest mammals in the world. It contains plants without roots and animals which have adapted to living completely submerged underwater for part of the day and exposed completely to air for the rest of the day.

In addition, the seashore and lakeshore both serve as habitats for species of birds found nowhere else. A study of the effects of the sun and moon upon bodies of water assumes dramatic importance when observed along a seashore or lakeshore. Finally, there is hardly a better place to observe the principles of erosion as the sea constantly tears away the land in one place only to build it up again with the same material in another place.

The seashore offers countless opportunities for studies, activities, and the integration of many subject areas including science (experimenting to see that most forms of life found in salt water cannot survive in fresh water and vice versa and why), art (making jewelry from shells), mathematics (observing geometric shapes in shells), and music (making musical instruments from shells similar to those made by the American Indians).

Other Resources

There are numerous other resources both in and around a community which offer rich opportunity for direct learning experiences. A few of the more common types are:

United States Weather Station: A branch of the weather bureau is usually located in every major airport and large city throughout the country. The weather station affords an excellent opportunity for teachers and students to observe first hand the instruments used to record and predict weather conditions.

Sewage Disposal Plant: It is here that students learn what happens to a city's sewage; how it is transformed through chemical processes into harmless material, and how the water, now relatively clean, is returned to the earth. The immense and urgent problem of water pollution becomes more significant to the student once he has visited a sewage disposal plant.

Construction and Stone Quarry Sites: Breaking ground for a new building, a new roadbed, or removing stone affords pupils the opportunity of observing and studying geologic features of the earth's surface which ordinarily would not be exposed. Sedimentary formations and other geologic features may be observed, along with various forms of rocks, minerals, and in some instances, even fossils.

Planetarium: The study of astronomy becomes more meaningful to students when they are given an opportunity to visit a planetarium. The complicated mechanism used for projecting the heavens on the dome of the planetarium provides an opportunity for many areas of study concerned with the universe. Many cities now have planetariums which schools take advantage of through field trips.

Aquarium: Many species of marine life, both plant and animal, which may not be readily available for observation and study at the local seashore, are found in aquariums. A well-planned aquarium, like a well-planned zoological park, can offer many educational opportunities to the alert teacher.

Lakes, Rivers, and Ponds: Each of these resources have features which are unique. There are various forms of animal and plant life peculiar to ponds and not present in lakes and rivers, and vice versa. Lakes, rivers, and ponds contain a wide variety of natural phenomena to be observed and studied by students.

Water Purification Plants: Understanding the source of water, the problems of getting it to the consumer, the purification processes, and the need for conservation can all be studied at the community's water plant. All students should be given the opportunity to visit their local plant.

Miscellaneous Resources: Other resources which offer opportunities for supplementing a school's program include:

Fish markets
Vegetable markets
Vacant lots
Backyards
Pet shops
Florist shops
Historical landmarks
Lumber mills
Manufacturing plants

Not to be overlooked are the granite base and marble lobbies of some public buildings; gold, silver, and diamond rings on display in jewelry stores; visiting certain neighborhoods to observe many varieties of animals on display in food stores which are favored by people of different national origins. Such food items may include octopus, squid, snails, rattlesnake meat, and fried grasshoppers.

Resources Provided by Federal Legislation

Open-space land program. As a result of the tremendous population increase the Federal Open-Space Land Program came into being to help counteract the rapid decline of open-space land for recreational and educational purposes. The program is the responsibility of the Urban Renewal Administration. In the first three years of the program, the Urban Renewal Administration approved of 220 grants which resulted in the purchase of over 100,000 acres of open land.

In order to help both state and local governments to take immediate action in the acquisition of open-space land for long range development programs, grants have been made by the Urban Renewal Administration of up to thirty percent of the cost of purchase of undeveloped land. For an urban area to take advantage of the program, several conditions must be met. The use of the land as open space must dovetail with the over-all plan of land use in the particular area; second, the land must be predominantly undeveloped; third, it must be open to the public, if feasible; and fourth, it must be land that is in excess of what would have ordinarily been provided. If, for example, a school district desires to cooperate with a park district in the development of a park-school, and if the land obtained exceeds the community's standard site requirements, then the local government would be eligible for a grant to purchase the additional land.[6]

Land and water conservation fund act. The Federal Land and Water Conservation Fund Act became law in 1964. The Act makes it possible, on a pay-as-you-go basis, for grants to be made for the procurement of land for recreational and conservation purposes by the Federal, state, and local governments. The Fund provides up to fifty percent for the acquisition of land and for water recreation development. The program is administered by the Bureau of Outdoor Recreation.

Wilderness act. One of the most significant legislative acts to be passed, manifesting extreme national concern for our rapidly disappearing wilderness areas, was the Wilderness Act (1964). The Wilderness Bill set aside over nine million acres of the last virgin areas located throughout the country. The bill had been bitterly opposed for many years by various commercial enterprises, including mining and lumber operations, and by other vested interest groups. Compromises had to be made before the bill could be

---

[6] *Recreation Newsletter* (Washington, D.C.: Recreation Division of the American Association for Health, Physical Education, and Recreation, November 1964), II, No. 1, pp. 1, 4.

passed. The bill is designed to protect for all time the last of the vast Federally-owned wilderness areas in the United States from our ever advancing civilization. The widely scattered lands have become part of a National Wilderness System.

According to the Act, the term "wilderness" is defined as ". . . an area where the earth and its community of life are untrammeled by man, where man himself is a visitor who does not remain . . . An area of undeveloped Federal land retaining its primeval character and influence, without permanent improvements of human habitation, which is protected and managed so as to preserve its natural conditions." In keeping with this definition, the construction of permanent buildings and the use of automobiles are not permitted in the protected areas. Motorboats and airplanes, to the consternation of many conservationists and other lovers of the outdoors, are permitted to operate in those areas where they were permitted to operate before passage of the bill. If the President of the United States believes it to be in the national interest, he may cause the removal of wilderness areas from Federal protection.

Despite the compromises which had to be made, the people of the nation are at least assured that there will forever remain areas in the country where one may seek tranquillity, even if only for a little while, away from the complexities of civilization, where one may learn nature's secrets, and where one may find precious time to be reminded of the rejuvenating effects of looking upon a world of untouched natural beauty which once upon a time covered our entire land.

It has been seen in this chapter that any school system, interested in developing an outdoor education program, has a variety of resources at its disposal. There are relatively few, if any, communities in the country which can boast of having all, or even most, of the resource facilities described here; nevertheless, every community has enough to introduce a program of outdoor education. What is really needed is motivated leadership that is able to make the most of what is available in the community.

CHAPTER V

Leadership for Outdoor Education

Leadership is the most important factor in a successful outdoor education program. Although the quality of outdoor resources is important, without dynamic leadership, the best resources become ineffective.

Despite the somewhat rapid but sporadic growth of outdoor education programs in the United States, most school teachers lack sufficient preparation to assume leadership responsibilities in this new area. Consequently, many teachers are reluctant to make use of the educational resources of the outdoors for the enrichment of their programs.

Yet outdoor education, it should be emphasized again, is not a subject in itself; rather, it is primarily a learning tool which cuts across all disciplines as has been noted in Chapter III. Because it is not a separate discipline, no special teacher certification is required. All that a teacher needs in order to be eligible to teach outdoor education is interest, enthusiasm, eagerness to attempt new learning techniques, and a willingness to give up her role as an omniscient pedagogue and show a desire to learn along with the students. Many teachers, because of their own interest in camping and outdoor education, and as a result of their own initiative, have had rich and valuable experiences in this area through participation in summer children's camps, and courses and workshops at colleges and universities. These teachers, despite a lack of formal preparation, provide the resource for schools to start an outdoor education program.

Qualifications and Competencies for Outdoor Education Leaders

Although the authors attempt to point out in this book that supplementing the classroom curriculum with teaching in the outdoors is not as difficult a task as many teachers may believe, the reader should not assume that outdoor education requires no special qualifications and competencies. On the contrary, outdoor education demands even more from a teacher than usual classroom teaching. For one thing, maintaining discipline in an outdoor education program while attempting at the same time to keep the learning atmosphere on an informal basis, requires a particular type of leadership ability. There are some teachers who are not able to adapt to this type of teaching, while others adapt quite readily.

Smith, Carlson, Donaldson, and Masters list the following leadership requirements for those involved in outdoor education, especially with young people:

1. A knowledge of human growth and development which helps teachers and leaders understand (a) the nature of learning in informal and life-like situations; and (b) the behavior of children and youth in out-of-classroom settings, particularly in the outdoor environment.
2. Competence in teaching methods in informal outdoor settings, and an ability to relate such learning to classroom objectives and activities.
3. A general knowledge of the outdoor environment and the nature of outdoor activities, with competencies in outdoor interpretation and the teaching of outdoor skills.[1]

Because school camping has assumed an important role in many school systems engaged in outdoor education programs, qualifications and competencies for leadership in a school camp will be emphasized in this section.

School camp administrator. The director of a school camp has many responsibilities which necessitate that great care be taken in the selection of the person to administer the program. Trillingham suggests:

> The camp director's qualifications should be consistent with those required for a good school administrator who has had considerable experience in camping and outdoor education and who loves to work with people. He should have excellent administrative ability with a sound educational philosophy and a genuine belief in democratic principles and democratic administration. The camp director should welcome, develop and maintain new ideas, and recognize possible program changes and developments for himself and staff. A good camp director should have a knowledge of business techniques, particularly in purchasing and ordering. If possible he should have previous experience as a counselor in a school camping and outdoor

---

[1] Smith, Carlson, Donaldson, and Masters, *Outdoor Education,* p. 247.

> education program. He should have a general interest in and knowledge of the growth and development of children.[2]

Clarke further supports the importance of the proper selection of the school camp administrator:

> The director of the school camp is a decisive factor in its program, for he sets the tone and shapes the developing plan of activities. The camp's program becomes a direct reflection of the understanding and ability of the director. His qualifications should include administrative ability, an understanding of democratic procedure and a belief in it, and, most important, an understanding of the problems of human relations. It is desirable that the camp director have experience in public school teaching and in administration. Teaching experience is helpful to him, since the school program and the camp program must complement each other.[3]

Smith, Carlson, Donaldson, and Masters suggest that the camp administrator be designated as the coordinator:

> The coordinator should have administrative ability in addition to being well versed in curriculum practices and child development principles. Outdoor skills and a general knowledge of camp administration are desirable. The position requires versatility, for the coordinator usually becomes a combination of administrator, teacher and handyman.[4]

In her study involving qualifications for camp leadership, Brown cites the qualifications, which the director of a children's summer camp should possess. The authors consider that the qualifications apply equally well to the administrator of a school camp or outdoor education center. Most of the qualifications are similar to those which any able administrator should possess, except for the following which are unique abilities that should be possessed by outdoor education administrators in particular:

> Understanding of camping goals.
> Understanding of basic health and safety principles, procedures and facts.
> Knowledge of materials and techniques in recreational leadership.
> Knowledge of activities concerned with living in the out-of-doors.[5]

---

[2] C. C. Trillingham, *Outdoor Education: A Handbook for School Districts* (Los Angeles, California: Office of the Superintendent of Schools, 1954), pp. 26–27.

[3] Clarke, *Public School Camping,* p. 39.

[4] Smith, Carlson, Donaldson, Masters, *Outdoor Education,* p. 104.

[5] Jean G. Brown, *Job Descriptions and Qualifications for Camp Leadership Positions,* p. 87.

Leaders (classroom teachers and/or counselors). In a school camp situation the responsibility for leadership and twenty-four-hour-a-day supervision represents greater work and more time than one teacher can handle. For each class of thirty pupils at least three counselors should be assigned. These may come from one of the following sources:

1. Other teachers from the school.
2. Seniors from high school.
3. College students performing field work or student teaching.
4. Qualified parents.
5. Volunteer citizens who possess special competencies in outdoor education.

Aside from the general competencies which a good teacher should have, one who will be teaching or serving as a counselor in a school camp should possess the following abilities: (The list is only partial. Refer to footnote No. 6 for complete list.)

1. An understanding of the underlying philosophy of school camping.
2. An understanding of the benefits derived from school camping in child development.
3. Skill in integrating pre-camp, camp, and post-camp experiences in the classroom so that the child has a continuing and total meaningful experience rather than a "one shot" isolated experience.
4. An ability to work effectively with groups and to provide children's groups with democratic experiences.
5. Skill in working with varying size groups in an informal setting and in the outdoors involving "techniques of group structuring."
6. An understanding of the philosophy inherent in work experiences and daily living chores and skill in incorporating such experiences in the camp program.
7. Familiarity with, and an understanding of, the natural world, outdoor living and conservation and skill in integrating these activities with the school curriculum through direct experiences.[6]

Whether the counselor in a school camp is a teacher or comes from some other background he should possess the following qualifications, according to Clarke:

> Cooperation, not competition, is the road to desirable attitudes within the camp staff. The counselor must have initiative, but must use this initiative as a member of a team. To achieve teamwork, the

[6] Berger, *A Plan for Developing Competencies for Leadership in School Camping,* pp. 126–128.

> counselor must practice cheerfulness, self-control, and a fundamental honesty with himself and with others . . .
>
> The counselor must be alive to the outdoors. The feeling of being at home in the outdoors and the pioneer's ability to find or create fun or interest regardless of conditions are essential. The counselor should know both the bounty and the limitations of the outdoors. He should be able to seek out its wonders and present his findings with meaning to youngsters. The counselor must be warm and responsive. He must be able to respond when a child is thrilled at the discovery of something the counselor sees every day. He must be sympathetic enough to sense the child's first pangs of homesickness and be able to discuss them. He must be capable of helping the camper to work through his problems to a happy experience providing new interests.[7]

In the Outdoor Education Handbook published by the Los Angeles County School District, California, the responsibility of the counselor is outlined:

> The counselor's primary responsibility in the school camping and outdoor education program is to guide the children in the planning, conducting, and evaluating experiences of the program. He should be a leader of children and have a genuine understanding of the child and respect for his individual personality. The camp counselor should be well educated as a teacher and have had classroom experience prior to being assigned to a position of leadership in the outdoor education program. It is desirable that the camp counselors be well prepared in the leadership of children and yet have some special preparation in one or more subject areas such as music, art, craft, or science. Additional personal qualifications that are desirable for well-educated counselors are:
>
> 1. Well-rounded personality, including being socially well-adjusted.
> 2. Maturity in judgment.
> 3. Emotional stability.
> 4. Willingness to assume responsibility.
> 5. Friendly and cooperative attitude.
> 6. Love of the out-of-doors.
> 7. Love of children.
> 8. Pleasant personal appearance.
> 9. Alertness to additional educational possibilities inherent in the program.[8]

---

[7] Clarke, *Public School Camping*, pp. 36–37.
[8] Trillingham, *Outdoor Education*, pp. 27–28.

Types of Leadership Arrangements

Specialists. There is a variety of leadership practices engaged in by different school camps. Some school systems prefer to hire a separate full-time staff of regular teachers who are well versed in outdoor education. This practice is usually carried on by the school system which owns or leases a camp and conducts programs on a year-around basis. In addition to the teachers, the school system may also engage counselors. The counselors in some cases may be parents of children who have already had a school camp experience. The counselors may also be high school students who have demonstrated leadership in the outdoors. In some school camps, the classroom teacher is assigned the role of counselor. The assigned teachers have the responsibility of conducting the various outdoor education activities while the counselors take over during rest periods, meal time, and bedtime, and also act as the disciplinarians during activities. There is somewhat of a cleavage between the duties of the camp teacher and the duties of the classroom teacher. In camp the classroom teacher usually plays the role of observer unless he possesses a specific ability relating to camping and outdoor education.

The arguments favoring the classroom teacher's role as observer are:

1. The classroom teacher, being relieved of major responsibilities, has an opportunity to observe students in a type of setting which will often reveal patterns of behavior not manifested in the formal atmosphere of a classroom.

2. The students receive a more significant experience in outdoor education, for the teachers who lead them are outdoor education specialists and know their subject matter thoroughly.

3. Since school camping is a twenty-four-hour-a-day responsibility, the teachers, as in the school system, need free time away from their students for relaxation; hence, the need for counselors.

The objections to the role of observer are:

1. One of the most justifiable arguments for school camping is that it complements the regular school curriculum. The school camping experience should be a continuation of the normal school curriculum transferred, but somewhat modified, into the outdoors, and later transferred back into the classroom. It should be a continuing experience involving discussions and study in the classroom

followed by practical, direct learning experiences in the outdoors. Only the classroom teacher knows her curriculum procedures thoroughly enough to effectively carry out the school camping experience as a total part of the school curriculum. The value of this experience is lost if the classroom teacher is assigned merely to the role of observer.

2. Outdoor education teacher specialists may be familiar with field science and related subjects but may be weak in academic content or creative or applied arts, such as social studies, art, and music, all of which are important in an outdoor education experience.

3. School camp provides the classroom teacher a unique opportunity to observe her students in a variety of informal settings. It is known that children react differently in different situations. They may react in one way during a field trip and differently at the dinner table or before bedtime. The classroom teacher should be involved with her students at these times in order to obtain a composite picture of the child. The cleavage between the teacher and the counselor hinders the above observation.

Teacher-counselor. Other school systems encourage the classroom teacher to take complete charge of her class in the outdoors but, more often than not, provide other teachers, including specialists, such as music, art, and science teachers to assist her in the program. In addition, the school administration may also supply counselors to relieve the teacher during rest periods and at other times.

In yet other school systems, the teacher is encouraged to coordinate the program but resource people, such as a state forester, a retired biologist, or a conservationist, are engaged to lead field trips and to otherwise cover the science-oriented areas with which the classroom teacher may not be as familiar.

Donaldson believes that school camps should favor general leadership rather than specialists. He says:

> Securing a staff which can live with children and learn with them is of critical importance. It poses the most difficult problem in organizing a camp. Many of the institutions which have trained camp counselors have provided personnel with rather highly developed specialties. Since good camping is hour-by-hour and day-by-day living, its guidance cannot be divided among a dozen specialists. Sympathetic, alert, curious, and vigorous men and women are required—interested in the *whole* child rather than in the direction of a specialized activity. . . .[9]

[9] Donaldson, *School Camping,* p. 95.

Thurston supports this viewpoint when he states:

> Basically, a qualified teacher-counselor is a good teacher who understands how children grow, develop, and learn, and one with a minimum of specialization in any phase of the camp program. Obviously, teaching in the camp and in the out-of-doors requires an approach, skills, and methods different from those often employed in the classroom. Since the outdoors becomes a laboratory for many learning experiences, the teacher needs general knowledge and acquaintance with the out-of-doors which can be attained through pre-service training and internship, but mostly through effective in-service training.[10]

Gilliland, in his study of administrative factors in establishing school camping programs, stated:

> A general program of education is the best type of training for teacher-counselors. Some experience in camping is desirable, however, a good teacher fits in with the camp program very quickly.[11]

Participation of the classroom teacher. Utilization of the classroom teacher as the principal leader in school camp programs is favored by most proponents of outdoor education. Smith, Carlson, Donaldson, and Masters have this to say:

> Ideally, the well prepared classroom teacher should be able to use the outdoors as effectively for teaching as the classroom and the library or any other facility for instruction. Modern-day teaching methods and the required preparation in subject matter should equip teachers to teach wherever the environment is most conducive to the learning objectives in question. The outdoors is free from the usual classroom props and traditional procedures. But skillful teaching should be found in the community laboratory as well as in the classroom. Too often teacher preparation and pre-service experiences have been related largely to the classroom and the teaching of abstractions.[12]

Freeberg and Taylor also suggest that in most cases the classroom teacher should provide the leadership necessary to the extent of planning and conducting outdoor education activities in instances where the experiences involved will make more meaningful the subject or subjects being taught.[13]

The inevitable question which arises at this point is: Should

---

[10] Thurston, *Community School Camping,* p. 37.
[11] Gilliland, *A Study of Administrative Factors,* p. 157.
[12] Smith, Carlson, Donaldson, and Masters, *Outdoor Education,* pp. 247–248.
[13] Freeberg and Taylor, *Programs in Outdoor Education,* p. 59.

teachers be compelled to attend school camp with their classes? The Tyler, Texas school camp bulletin has this to say:

> The answer is an emphatic "No!" The teacher who is not a camper and doesn't want to be one but who feels forced makes as poor a camper as does the child who is forced to attend. Our superintendent has guaranteed that no teacher should feel the least bit of pressure to go camping.[14]

On the other hand, there have been occasions when teachers who were reluctant to attend school camps, but were literally compelled to go, found the experience more enjoyable and educationally more stimulating than they anticipated.

The trend throughout the country appears to be that utilization of classroom teachers in outdoor education programs is essential to a successful program.

Coordinating the School Staff via the Interdisciplinary Approach

Although the classroom teacher, according to most authorities, should be the key person in an outdoor education program, she still needs the assistance of other school staff members. More and more instructional staffs are working cooperatively through new teaching techniques and curriculum organizations such as team teaching, core courses, and block plans and applying these techniques and methods to outdoor education. There are opportunities in outdoor education for the team approach which involves teachers whose qualifications and interests are of such a variety that they complement one another. Staffs from social studies, health education, music, art, recreation, homemaking, language arts, physical education, and science can make significant contributions to the total program. By doing this, the classroom teacher has available special resource people, to enrich the outdoor education learning experiences for students. At the same time, the team staff personnel act as resources for each other. This interdisciplinary approach is used in a number of colleges and universities which operate field campuses, camps, and outdoor education centers.

---

[14] Donaldson, *School Camping,* pp. 137–138.

Problems Associated with Recruitment of Classroom Teachers as Outdoor Leaders

Unfortunately, teacher education for the most part has not recognized a definite responsibility for preparing teachers to assume leadership in outdoor education. Lack of preparation is a major reason which causes many teachers to be dubious of making use of the outdoor environment for the enrichment of curriculums.

Fear of teaching outdoors. Many classroom teachers are reluctant to leave the formal atmosphere of the classroom to go into the informal atmosphere of an unfamiliar outdoor environment. Some harbor the fear that because of their unfamiliarity with the natural environment, they will not be able to adequately answer their students' questions concerning certain natural phenomena. This uncertainty may be used to advantage. The teacher can stimulate the student to search out the answer. If the student is compelled to discover the necessary information for himself, in the course of his studies he may find other interesting related facets for further exploration.

Another possible advantage in not being able to supply answers to all problems is that the students see the teacher as a fallible human being who is not omniscient. Many children make a distinction between teachers and people. When school closes at the end of the day, the teacher goes into never-never land while everyone else goes home. Teachers simply don't drink, gamble, or become involved in emotional entanglements. They only teach. The teacher who assumes the role of an ordinary person enters into a much more realistic and normal relationship with the students. A teacher must have the courage to say "I don't know," and sufficient interest in her students to say "But let's see if we can find the answer."

A knowledge of the outdoors is, of course, important in an outdoor education program. School administrators, however, must be realistic and realize that many classroom teachers simply do not possess this knowledge. But a good teacher, one well versed in effective teaching techniques and a normal amount of curiosity, can learn enough about the outdoors in a relatively short time to provide her class, with perhaps some aid from resource people, with a meaningful and memorable outdoor education experience.

Preparing Classroom Teachers for Outdoor Education Programs

What schools are doing. School administrators have helped to allay their teachers' fears through several approaches. Some schools conduct in-service education programs, experimental and pilot programs, employing their own science personnel and other resource people. Resident school camp experience is usually delayed; instead, local trips are encouraged, which may go no further than the boundaries of the school property. In some schools the science supervisor prepares helpful written material concentrating on local areas of interest. Also, the classroom teacher has access to reference books dealing with science, conservation, and nature activities.

In addition to their own teachers, many school systems seek resource personnel from the surrounding community, from organizations interested in outdoor activities, and from the state and Federal governments. Such resource personnel, adequately screened, complement the school's outdoor education program by broadening the educational program and, on occasion, providing more depth to the various activities. Gilliland supports this view:

> How to use resource personnel in the local program deserves careful consideration. When we speak of utilizing resource people, we refer to hobbyists, specialists, conservationists and others . . . It is common practice to secure help from many groups with related interests. Resource people from these groups usually are happy to participate in a school camp program and make an excellent contribution.[15]

Sources for personnel. School systems embarking upon an ambitious outdoor education program can, and do, draw upon qualified resource personnel found in almost every community. Many people have hobbies related to the outdoors and are well acquainted with their particular interest. Retired people are not to be overlooked; they spend time with their avocation and may be quite knowledgeable in their field of interest. Almost every county has access to a federal government office representing forestry and agriculture. Personnel from these offices cooperate often with local schools by assisting teachers in conducting outdoor education classes and leading field trips.

---

[15] Gilliland, *School Camping,* pp. 48–49.

Caution should be taken when dealing with consultants and resource personnel who are not also teachers. Some potential resource personnel may be well versed in a subject, yet may not be capable of adequately projecting their knowledge to others. These experts, however, are still utilized by school systems in the capacity of consultants to the classroom teachers. Resource personnel can contribute more to the program when they share in the planning of outdoor education programs. By such participation they are better equipped to assist in carrying out the objectives of the program.

The classroom teacher can also receive help through voluntary community study committees, which a number of schools have. Among the functions of such a committee are the conduct of an inventory of local community resources to identify places for field trips and names of local resource people; and the procurement of information and materials for the conduct of the program.

Local consultants and resource leaders should be encouraged to participate in local workshops and clinics for the benefit of teachers. Teachers need these direct learning experiences in the outdoors before they can be expected to conduct such programs themselves. Local camps, parks, and other outdoor areas can be utilized for field trips and for skills clinics, such as in outdoor cooking techniques, for example.[16]

What schools can do. One major solution to the leadership problem is for schools to arrange scholarships for teachers to enroll in an off-campus course or in other courses in outdoor education offered by universities. There are a number of such off-campus courses and workshops conducted by over fifty universities and colleges throughout the country. See Chapter II, pages 29 to 30 for a description of some of these programs.

There are also numerous national organizations—private, professional, and governmental which offer in-service programs conducted by experts in conservation, recreation, outdoor sports, and other fields. The American Camping Association sponsors both regional and national workshops for leaders interested in outdoor education. Michigan State University, in cooperation with the Outdoor Education Project of the American Association of Health, Physical Education, and Recreation, conducts a summer outdoor education workshop at the University's W. K. Kellogg Gull Lake Biological Station in Michigan.

---

[16] Smith, Carlson, Donaldson, and Masters, *Outdoor Education,* p. 278.

The National Audubon Society operates a number of nature and conservation camps for teachers and youth leaders during the summer months. Activities cover the study of all natural resources and projects which the participants can use with those whom they will be teaching. The course lasts for approximately two weeks and is repeated several times during the summer months. The camps are located in Connecticut, Maine, Wisconsin, and Wyoming.

Some state conservation departments have accepted the responsibility to prepare leaders in outdoor education. A number of colleges and universities have worked out arrangements with state conservation departments to offer courses and in-service training in science and conservation. There are some conservation departments that conduct conservation activities during the summer months for teachers. The State Department of Conservation in Michigan conducts weekend workshops for teachers during the school year at its Conservation School. In addition to developing interests and skills in the outdoors, the teachers also help plan outdoor education programs for their own schools.[17]

Another solution to supplying leadership is to relieve a teacher who is interested in outdoor education from all or part of teaching responsibilities to visit school districts which conduct programs. The same teacher could be assigned to initiate a similar program in her own school district. The teacher, ideally, should have little or no classroom responsibilities in order to give her complete freedom to develop an outdoor education program. Some school districts such as Newton, Massachusetts and Edgemont, New York have hired full-time teachers who are well versed in outdoor education to develop outdoor education programs for their school systems.

Outdoor education and teacher training. One major solution to obtaining adequate leadership among teachers is to attack the problem at its source—teachers' colleges and departments of education in other colleges and universities. The New Jersey State Department of Education has a requirement that students in all state teachers colleges must spend one week at the New Jersey State School of Conservation. Over two thousand education majors each year participate in an outdoor education program at the State's School of Conservation. In addition, students from some twenty-five

---

[17] Smith, Carlson, Donaldson, and Masters, *Outdoor Education*, p. 272.

public schools come to the School of Conservation for a week of school camping.

At the present time there are relatively few university and college education departments in the country which do much more than offer a few courses in the basic sciences, with hardly any offering courses in outdoor education.

Outline for outdoor education curriculum. Outdoor education programs in the schools would undoubtedly expand more rapidly if more colleges and universities, specifically teacher education institutions, would include outdoor education in their curricula.

Some educators believe that leadership training in outdoor education should not be offered as a separate course, but integrated into the regular college curriculum. Use of the outdoors should occur when it would serve to make a particular course of study more meaningful. Other educators feel that specialized courses in outdoor education should be developed and incorporated into the general college curriculum, while still others believe that a separate course of study in outdoor education should be developed.

The following outline might be used for either developing specialized courses in outdoor education which could be included in existing curricula, or for developing a course of study in outdoor education.

Introduction to Outdoor Education

(Extent of outdoor education programs in the United States and in Europe, philosophies, objectives, job opportunities, and a description of organizations related to outdoor education)

Techniques of Outdoor Education Leadership

Principles of Organization and Administration in Outdoor Education

(Design, construction, and maintenance of outdoor education plants and facilities, organizing outdoor education experiences, public relations, recruiting staff, developing budgets, bookkeeping, legal problems, and other administrative functions)

Planning and Design of Outdoor Education and Recreation Facilities

Relating Outdoor Education Experiences to the School Curriculum

Administration Accounting

Independent Study—Senior Project

Choose one of the following: plan and develop a nature trail; plan an outdoor education center, showing various types of facilities; plan an outdoor education program for a sixth grade class; plan an outdoor education program for a high school class.

Procedures for Teaching Outdoor Science for Elementary Teachers
Procedures for Teaching Outdoor Science for Secondary Teachers
Mathematics in the Outdoors
Introduction to Geology
Introduction to Astronomy
Introduction to Meteorology and Climatology
Introduction to General Biology
Introduction to General Ecology
Introduction to Field Zoology
Introduction to Plant Science
Introduction to Entomology
Introduction to Herpetology
Introduction to Ornithology
Conservation of Natural Resources
Introduction to Wildlife Management
Introduction to Forest Management
Introduction to Aquatic Biology
Techniques and Safety Procedures for Hunting and Fishing
Techniques and Safety Procedures for Boating
Arts and Crafts—Its Place in Outdoor Education

The student should take the general education courses required by the college or university as well as the core courses in teacher education.

Student teaching in school camps. A number of teacher education institutions and university and college education departments recently have worked out cooperative arrangements in outdoor education with school districts, thus giving student teachers an opportunity to gain practical experience in this area. In such school districts, the student may spend a week or longer doing student teaching and observing in a school camp.

At Northern Illinois University students who major in education take part in outdoor education experiences at the University's Lorado Taft Field Campus, including an actual school camp session.

Student teachers from Michigan State University in the past have spent a week in outdoor education programs at the Clear Lake Camp. Outdoor education experiences are provided student teachers at Southern Illinois University in cooperation with the College of Education and the Outdoor Education Department. Other universities conducting similar programs are Wayne University, Eastern Michigan University, Western Michigan University, and New York University.

Student internships. A most significant approach to providing better trained teachers for outdoor education is for students to participate as interns in outdoor education programs. At Antioch College, internships are part of the college's regular work-study program. Cooperative arrangements have been made between Antioch and a number of school systems throughout the country to employ education and science majors as interns in outdoor education centers and school camps for as long as six months.

School systems and universities which have cooperated with Antioch College in this internship program are: Cleveland Heights, Ohio; Battle Creek, Michigan; San Diego and Long Beach, California; Dearborn, Michigan; Boston University; and New York University. Antioch College also maintains its own outdoor education center on a one thousand acre plot of land. Here, school districts participate in school camping experiences. Antioch students are employed by the center to give them practical training in outdoor education. Other types of outdoor education programs are conducted at the center for the benefit of the college's own students and others preparing to be leaders in outdoor education. During the summer months, the college conducts a school camp workshop for teachers. Other colleges having internship programs are the State University of New York at Cortland, Springfield College in Massachusetts, and Pennsylvania State University.

Colleges and universities preparing leaders in outdoor education should provide a variety of educational experiences. By its very nature, outdoor education necessitates that leadership preparation must involve not one but many departments of a college or university, if students are to be effective teachers in the outdoors. Departments of psychology, sociology, biology, zoology, geology, education, physical science, mathematics, English, physical education, health, recreation, music, art, history, agriculture, and forestry have a contribution they can make and students in these courses could all benefit by an outdoor education experience.

Suggested steps for development of leadership at local level. Following is a general plan which school administrators may follow in setting up a teacher preparation program for outdoor education leadership:

1. Make an inventory of teachers in the school system who have had some experience in outdoor-related activities and who possess specific outdoor skills.
2. Have the science supervisor prepare written material about nat-

ural phenomena in the local area and provide a bibliography of writings in outdoor education.

3. Obtain elementary books dealing with natural history, nature lore, and conservation and make them accessible to the teachers.
4. Form a committee of teachers, with or without laymen, whose functions would be to take an inventory of local resources—places to take field trips, museums in the area, names of resource people, and availability of written material in outdoor education.
5. Develop in-service education programs—workshops and clinics for teachers with the aid of a qualified staff member to coordinate the program with resource personnel. Don't overlook the county agriculture agent, local forester, and fishing and hunting organizations. Another excellent source for resource personnel is the local college or university.
6. Encourage teachers from different disciplines to form committees to study ways in which all of the disciplines can be integrated into a unified and total outdoor education program.
7. Encourage teachers taking graduate work to include as electives courses in outdoor education.
8. Request that school boards provide scholarships for teachers who wish to attend a summer outdoor education course or workshop.
9. Encourage teachers to visit local nature centers, junior museums, museums of natural history, and outdoor education programs conducted in other communities.
10. Encourage teachers to make local field trips with their classes. They may not have to go any further than the boundary of the school property for the field trips.

There is considerable written material, charts, aids, and films dealing with aspects of outdoor education available for teachers. See the Appendix in this book for a list of the various sources of information.

This chapter has attempted to illustrate that no outdoor education program can be successful without capable leadership, regardless of the wealth of natural resources and excellent facilities which might be available.

This chapter has also attempted to show that while there is a need for more adequate leadership for outdoor education programs, steps can and are being taken by schools to train their own teachers for the leadership needed. In the interim, more and more colleges and universities, aware of the importance of outdoor education are developing programs designed to provide leaders who are well-equipped in the field of outdoor learning.

CHAPTER VI

Initiating an Outdoor Education Program

The absence of information on how to start a program of outdoor education or school camping is one of the major factors contributing to the hesitancy of school administrators to initiate such programs. Among the obstacles, State Departments of Education have not produced syllabi or instructions to local school districts and few textbooks or teacher's manuals exist.

A study of the administrative problems was conducted by John Gilliland in 1949.[1] He identified twelve problems which schools must overcome in the process of getting a program started.

1. *Developing Interest:* Administrators, teachers, students, and parents must have an awareness of the values inherent in an outdoor education program before a program can be initiated.

2. *Planning the Program:* In order to assure positive outcomes, careful planning must precede the actual carrying out of any outdoor education program.

3. *Selecting the Staff:* Few teachers have been prepared, through work taken at college, for leadership in outdoor education programs. This is one of the principal reasons administrators delay starting a program. Until teacher education schools begin to assume a more direct responsibility for preparing teachers for this new field, progress will be slow.

4. *Providing for Health and Safety:* The health of a child is always of primary concern to parents. Will their children be safe and be in a healthful environment? Their anxiety about these things influences the attitude of the school administrator.

5. *Financing the Program:* Anything new that adds to the school's budget tends to meet with resistance from the members of a Board of Education. However, many programs have been started at no cost to the school system. Students earn their own money to cover expenses.

6. *Developing Leadership:* When the teaching staff is lacking in competency in the areas involving outdoor education, a program of

[1] John Gilliland, "A Study of the Administrative Factors in Establishing a Program of School Camping" (Doctoral thesis, New York University, 1949).

in-service training is in order. A substitute for such training would be attendance at one of the outdoor education leadership training institutes conducted by some universities.

7. *Interpreting School Camping to the Community:* An important step in initiating an outdoor education program is to acquaint the community with the purposes and objectives of the program. This may be accomplished through PTA meetings, planned visits by parents to the school camp, or other outdoor education activity.

8. *Acquiring a Camp Site:* Often a difficult step in starting a program of school camping is locating a suitable camp facility. Distance from school, cost, and adequacy of the site for conducting a program of activities are the major criteria which should be used to evaluate a potential site.

9. *Providing Facilities:* Providing the type of buildings and program areas often presents a problem to a school system. All children's camps do not possess the kinds of facilities which are essential to an effective program. When these are missing they need to be developed. A place for science and nature study is required. Also important is indoor work space with adequate resource material. Comfortable, safe, and healthy living units are necessary for the welfare of students.

10. *Organizing for Administration:* A special committee or advisory council composed of school board members, school administrators, community officials, teachers, and parents should be established to guide the development of a new program of outdoor education or school camping.

11. *Providing for Business Management:* It is just as necessary to provide for efficient business management for the school camp as it is for the regular school. Periodic financial reports on the camp operation should be prepared and made public.

12. *Meeting Legal Problems:* There is probably no other problem confronting the school administrator that results in delaying the start of an outdoor education program more than the question of the school's legal authority to conduct such a program. Some states have specific laws permitting school districts to acquire camp sites and conduct programs. In other states the authority is implied in more general legal statutes.

The Organization and Administration of Outdoor Education Programs

In schools where outdoor education has been developed it has been largely a question of finding a person best qualified and interested to coordinate and conduct the program. This person might be a science, a social studies, or a physical education teacher. Outdoor education is interdisciplinary and as such is best administered when it is not attached to a subject area department.

The trend that appears to be developing in this country is the assignment of a person as coordinator at the community or district level. He may be assigned fulltime or on a seasonal basis depending on the scope of the program and he works with a faculty committee of various subject matter teachers and one or more principals to help to develop the program. He reports directly to the Superintendent or to one of his assistants.

The use of advisory groups. Some school systems conducting outdoor education programs have advisory groups which include parents and interested citizens. These groups have considerable public relations value and help to develop support for the program. They also help to make areas and facilities available to the school.

Legal provisions. The school laws of most states make it possible for the conduct of programs in outdoor education. Only a few states, most notably New York, Michigan, and California, have specific school camp laws. Eventually, all states should enact appropriate legislation for the conduct of school camps and outdoor education programs. The laws should embody the following elements:

1. Authorization to establish camps on property obtained by purchase, lease, or gift, within and outside of the school district.
2. Authorization for joint operation of a camp by two or more school districts.
3. Authorization for the use of school funds and for fees for food and other expenses.
4. Authorization to use nonteaching personnel as resource leaders in the program.
5. Specific authorization to conduct programs outside the state.

Financing the program. Outdoor education programs obviously need financing. Field trips involving various subject areas are usually estimated and budgeted a year in advance. They seldom run into budgetary obstacles. On the other hand, school camping involving a resident experience in a camp setting, usually requires a special budget. However, some programs have been completely financed by parents, or by the pupils who earn the camp fee by working on community or home projects. In other situations there is a sharing of cost between parents and the school board, with the parents paying for the food cost and the board meeting all other expenses.

In some communities part of the budget for outdoor education programs is supported by parent-teacher associations or civic groups. Yet to be resolved in most states is the question of whether funds allocated to local communities by the state for general education purposes might be used to finance outdoor education programs.

At the beginning of a new program the cost should be kept to the minimum. As greater involvement of pupils occur the cost will go up. The usual items which must be budgeted for in the operation of a school camping program, whether they are included within the total school budget or in a separate, special budget, are:

1. Rental or purchase of a camp site. In some instances this may be obtained without a fee from the state, county, or municipality.
2. Food service.
3. Transportation.
4. Instruction and leadership.
5. Insurance.
6. Supplies and equipment.
7. Operation and maintenance, when not included in the rental fee.

If a school district purchases property for development of a permanent outdoor education area, funds for capital improvement will be necessary.

First Stages of an Outdoor Education Project

It does not take much to get a program of outdoor education started. As a matter of fact, most schools already have some aspect of a program in progress. It may be in the form of an outdoor club, winter ski club, science club, or field trips organized by classroom teachers.

There is no blueprint for starting an outdoor education program that is appropriate for every community. No two programs in existence today had the same beginning. From the study of several hundred programs the authors have concluded that the following ten steps could successfully launch a program of outdoor education in a school system.

1. Select a person who is interested and qualified to coordinate the program. This is an important step; no program will survive unless direction and leadership are given to it.

2. Prepare a concept statement and policy on outdoor education which has the approval of the school's administration. This is best achieved through a committee or council composed of teachers, administrators, and interested laymen.

3. Develop a general content outline of an outdoor education program. This should be accomplished by the coordinator with the cooperation of the outdoor education committee, or council, and subject matter specialists.

4. Conduct an inventory of the resources available for outdoor education in the community and surrounding area, up to one hundred miles from the community. The data thus collected will help determine the potential areas for study.

5. Identify resource persons in the community who possess certain specialized abilities which might be utilized in the program.

6. Recruit, select, and prepare leadership for the program. Teachers are generally not professionally prepared to teach in the out-of-doors. Thus, it becomes necessary, through in-service courses and field trips, to train the teachers who will be involved in the program.

7. Develop administrative procedures for:

   (a) System-wide organization of the program.
   (b) Liability protection for the student and the teacher involved in the program.
   (c) Health and accident insurance coverage for students.
   (d) Financing the program.
   (e) Food service.
   (f) Health and safety.

8. Inform parents and other citizens through an effective public relations program about the objectives of the program and how it will be conducted.

9. Evaluate the program periodically. Program improvement and justification will only be achieved through carefully planned evaluative studies.

10. Make an annual report to school administrators and to the community.

Every state education department should develop a positive policy statement on outdoor education in order that local school districts might be motivated and guided in this new field.

In summary, a functional formula for the initiation of a program of outdoor education might be stated as follows: Interest on the part of someone in the school system, plus a sympathetic administration, plus adequate preliminary planning will yield a program of outdoor education.

CHAPTER VII

Outdoor Education Activities and Projects

It is through activities and projects that the full value of an outdoor education program manifests itself. Regardless of the level of intelligence almost everyone can see, touch, taste, smell, or hear the natural world and, through these sense perceptions, learn. It has been demonstrated through personal experiences of teachers whom the authors have known that some children who do not respond effectively to classroom instruction achieve when placed in an informal setting such as that offered in an outdoor education program.

Some children may have excellent manual dexterity in constructing bird houses and bird feeders, or they may be unusually resourceful in adapting to outdoor living in the woods, and yet be labeled as slow learners in the classroom. The very bright and sometimes overconfident student, when exposed to the natural world, may discover that there is much to be learned. Outdoor activities aid in fulfilling many of the basic needs of children—achievement, recognition, satisfaction, and security, which, in turn, contribute to the development of the whole child—physically, socially, intellectually, and emotionally. Children, regardless of their capacity for learning, can gain through outdoor education experiences.

Although outdoor education programs are most effectively conducted in an informal atmosphere, the classroom teacher must not assume that careful planning is unnecessary. Unfortunately, this assumption is held by a number of teachers to the detriment of further development of outdoor education in their schools. Consideration must be given to the purpose and objectives for participating in specific activities, and how the activities will be conducted. Advance preparation for outdoor education is extremely important. Furthermore, a follow-up of the classes' outdoor experiences is also absolutely essential. This helps to reinforce what has been learned, and invariably results in further understanding of the activity. School camping programs which do not include advance preparation and follow-up of student experiences back in the classroom are invariably a waste of school time. Finally, the teacher and class need to evaluate their experience in the light of objectives they originally set for themselves.

Field Trips

The field trip, which is probably the most popular type of outdoor education program, serves as an excellent medium for pupil exposure to many stimulating experiences. The field trip offers opportunity for observing natural phenomena and collecting a variety of specimens.

General field trips. One of the most popular types of field trip activities is the general introduction to the outdoors. A little bit of everything is explored—evidence of soil erosion, rock outcroppings, a beaver dam, insects found beneath the bark of a dead tree, animal tracks, etc. With proper planning general field trip activities effectively serve as the gateway to the wonders found in the natural world, and help to motivate students to study in more detail the natural environment. One danger of the general field trip is that many teachers use it as the only type of outdoor experience for their pupils. Every excursion taken becomes general in nature. The student absorbs a great deal of fragmented bits of information which are difficult to relate. Fundamental principles of life and broad concepts rarely, if ever, become apparent.

Field trips with a theme. The field trip which has a specific theme avoids the errors of the general trip. More and more the emphasis on the part of the teachers is to center the trip around one or two specific objectives or themes. Some examples of themes for field trips are: "How Water, Wind, and Chemical Weathering Cause Erosion," "Construction Abilities of Animals," "How Plants Affect the Weather." The class is taken to a specific area which serves to demonstrate the particular theme chosen. For example, to point out how plants affect the weather, a trip is taken to a forest or wooded area, where a comparison may be made between the temperature on the edge of the forest and that within the forest. A previous discussion of the field trip as one of the outdoor education programs is in Chapter II, pages 20 to 21.

Nonscientific field trips. Field trips may include those serving to motivate students in art, music, poetry, and writing. How much more meaning and appreciation there is when one has walked through the woods—listening to the wind in the trees and the sounds of a bubbling brook—and then returning to the classroom and listening to Beethoven's "Pastorale" or "To a Water Lily" by Edward McDowall. Field trips are also taken by classes to study the history of a particular area. Visits might be made to abandoned farms to study soil conditions, the type of farming which had been carried on, the hardships encountered by the farmer and how nature is literally reclaiming the land. Old graveyards, Indian sites, abandoned mines, old lumber camps, and battlefields are other places of historical interest. Students can use the local library to locate helpful information about the history of the local area.

Conservation Projects

Conservation projects should not be conducted merely for their own sake if they are to be worthwhile educational experiences. The participants in any work project must first be made aware of the implications of the conservation of natural resources. A considerable amount of time needs to be spent on this topic for students to comprehend its significance. Once the student has had an exposure to the many problems involved in maintaining the country's natural resources, he may then be introduced to some conservation projects. It is best if the project selected serves a useful purpose. Usually the class need not go far afield; the school's property is often an excellent place to start. If there is a wooded area behind the school building it might need thinning in order to release the more vigorous and healthy saplings. Perhaps the soil is being washed away in certain areas of the school's small lawn due to a lack of sufficient vegetation. It may be necessary to do some planting—not only for erosion control but for beautification as well.

Bird sanctuary. The development of a small bird sanctuary on the school grounds is a project that produces quick results. A variety of plantings which offer both food and shelter, with the addition of bird feeders and bird houses constructed by the class, will result in many rewarding days for the students throughout the year. Bird feeders should be placed, if possible, under trees and near tall bushes. Birds, constantly alert to the dangers from the sky, hawks, for example, prefer to feed in areas where protection is close by.

Although developing a small wildlife sanctuary for birds is a conservation project, it is of more benefit to the people who build it than to the birds. The few birds that may be saved by bird feeders from starving during the winter months is of lesser value than the education and pleasure people derive from a bird feeding station. The sanctuary enhances learning of bird identification, gives those children who do well in manual skills a sense of accomplishment through constructing a bird feeder, and stimulates knowledge about bird behavior and the economic importance of birds to man.

Erosion control. One of the many advantages of outdoor education is the opportunity it provides to use flexible teaching methods. Learning need not always be a serious matter; it can also be treated as fun, which for many children may be the most effective method of learning.

Soil erosion is a vital aspect of outdoor education programs. Students develop a better understanding and appreciation of soil erosion when they have an opportunity to observe it and to correct it. Such a project, turned into a game for younger children, is here described. A group chances upon a small piece of land which is being eroded by rainwater due to lack of sufficient vegetation. This is an opportune time for the leader to open a discussion about the many ramifications of erosion. Plans are then made to prevent further erosion. If the group is not prepared to do "battle" with the "enemy," it may be necessary to return to the school or camp in order to obtain the necessary "weapons." This is also an opportune time to teach the children how to properly and safely use their "weapons."

Conservation projects, especially those which involve a young group of children, must be of such a nature that the group can soon see results of their efforts.

Citizenship education and conservation. Conservation projects are not only the province of elementary school age youngsters. There are more sophisticated projects in which high school students may participate. One high school teacher in his twelfth year citizenship education class gave his students the opportunity to select projects on conservation. The projects, all of a local nature, involved parks, water pollution, soil erosion, littering, and fish and game resources. One student decided to study the local trout streams and game resources. Other students in the class worked with the local sportsman's club to place conservation signs near feeder streams containing young trout. Still other students conducted a study of the local litter problem, particularly as it affected the local parks, and made recommendations for improvement. They also designed antilitter posters with the guidance of their art teacher. A map of the school's property and a long range planting program, including setting aside part of an area as a wildlife refuge containing a nature trail, were done by other students.

In the two examples discussed above—the efforts against soil erosion and litter—advantages of the activity method of learning was demonstrated. Each learning experience had a purpose and therefore it was meaningful to the student. The elementary age child, before he can fight soil erosion, first needs to learn how to use his tools properly. The high school student, before he can proceed further with his antilitter campaign, needs the advice from his art teacher to make his posters appealing so as to attract the attention of the community.

Miscellaneous Activities

The nature trail. Although it would be preferable for a school system to have a large natural area of ten acres or more on which to build a nature trail, it is by no means essential. Many principles and concepts involving natural phenomena can be effectively learned in a comparatively small area, provided those responsible for planning the trail are observant. As pointed out previously, quantity is not as important as quality when observations and studies are made of the natural world.

The planning of the nature trail is primarily the responsibility of the teacher or several teachers. Students, however, should participate, for they generally learn a great deal in the process of developing the trail. When planning a nature trail, professional help, along with help from local citizens who have an avocation in some phase of natural history, should be sought.

Many communities have Audubon Bird Clubs composed of people who are skilled in bird identification. They can be of great help in advising ways to attract wild birds along the nature trail or to a specific area. A member of the community knowledgeable in geology can help to identify the rocks and minerals along the trail. There may also be a local garden club whose members are familiar with wildflowers and who can help to identify them. Advice may also be obtained from the county agricultural agent and from the state forester.

Variety of trails. Schools lacking large acreages usually construct one general nature trail, that is, a nature trail which encompasses such studies as geology, biology, and conservation. If the school is fortunate enough to have a large natural area, it can then develop several nature trails, each with a different theme. One trail might emphasize the study of geology, including how rocks and minerals are formed, types of rocks and minerals, and the formation of the various features of the earth. Another trail might follow a brook. The stress could be on the various plants and animals which live alongside the brook with observations and studies made of various brook habitats—rapids, slack water, and pools.

Still another trail may concern itself primarily with soil—the various ways in which soil is formed; the effect which certain animals, such as earthworms, have upon the soil; what is meant by a watershed; and what happens to soil when the vegetation is removed. Although a trail might be designed for some specific purpose, this does not mean that other aspects of nature should not be included. The student should always be reminded of interrelationships among natural objects otherwise he may only learn to observe the trees, but never really see the wonders of the forest.

Many nature trails which have been developed include so-called "teaching stations." This means that pre-arranged areas, which contain something of particular interest, are located along the nature trail. The teaching station might consist of an unusual rock formation which may serve as an introduction to geology; or the station may feature soil erosion which can open the topic of conservation. The teaching station need not be static; that is, the same class should be able to walk along the trail more than once during the school year and see different objects each time. Some teaching stations should be chosen because they are constantly changing, for example, one with a good display of vegetation which changes as the seasons change. The area should show evidence of soil erosion. Dramatic changes can usually be observed in a comparatively short time. Many such stations can be developed which assure classes a new adventure every time they traverse the trail.

Labeling the trail. Several different techniques are used in the planning of nature trails. The most common is to place labels along the nature trail which identify such objects as wildflowers, mosses, ferns, and rocks and minerals. In heavily populated areas, or where there is a shortage of trained personnel to conduct trips, the trails are generally designed to be self-guiding. Usually, mimeographed booklets containing interesting facts about objects to be found along the way are located in a protected box at the beginning of the trail or are handed out by a staff member at the nature center or trailside museum. Objects are identified with numbers and the mimeographed booklets which are keyed to each number give detailed information about the objects. Another technique employed, and the one which the authors favor, is for the teacher to take a mimeographed booklet and encourage the children to find answers to questions raised. It is the feeling of some outdoor educators that, particularly among children, learning too often stops once an object has been identified.

"What tree is that?" "That's an oak tree." "What tree is that?" "That's a Ponderosa Pine." "What tree . . . ," and so on. The child is usually no longer interested once identification has taken place. The preferred technique is to delay identification and to interpret and relate interesting facts about the object. "This tree is used in the production of turpentine." "Notice how straight the branches of this shrub are." "The Indians fashioned arrows from them." When the child's curiosity has been aroused, the teacher may encourage him to return to class and obtain a key of trees, wildflowers, or whatever object needs to be identified and attempt to identify it himself. This is when true learning and better retention take place. "Pear Cactus," "Ironwood tree," "Yucca plant," "Columbine," "Quartz" . . . connecting these names with specific objects will, more than likely, be forgotten in a comparatively short time by most children. What appears to be of more lasting value, and what good teachers emphasize, are concepts such as the relationship of plants and animals in a desert environment, the soil and water holding ability of trees and other plants and what happens when these are cleared from the land, and the fact that the physical earth is constantly changing with mountains disappearing and being formed and the sea constantly eating away the land in one area while building it up in another. Thus, identifying an object appears to mean so much more and seems to result in more retention when the object is understood in its relationship with its environment.

When an adequate staff is available, personal tours are often arranged. In such cases it is common for the trails to be unlabeled. The personally conducted tour is generally superior to any other method, for questions may be raised which are not answered on the label or on the information sheet. In addition, personal contact with a naturalist or teacher on a nature trail appears to be more conducive to learning than exploration along a "self-guiding" nature trail which lacks such personal contact.

Nature by the square yard. As indicated previously, an outdoor education program can be carried out in a relatively small area. There is one activity involving no more than a square yard of land which can produce rewarding results. The activity becomes even more interesting when comparison studies are made with a wooded area, an open field, the edge of a marsh, or the edge of a wooded area. The procedure is to mark off a square yard of earth and examine with a magnifying glass the type of life contained in the area. A surprisingly large number of different species of plants, insects, and other small animals including spiders, worms, and slugs can be observed.

Stump scouting. This activity gives students excellent practice in making observations and deductions. The originator of this fascinating detective-type activity was William G. Vinal, well-known in outdoor education circles. All that is needed is the stump of a tree. The approximate age of a tree can be determined simply by counting the number of annual rings found in the stump; but considerably more may be learned than the age. The years during the life of a tree when there was little or much rain will be evident, as well as whether the tree was felled by an axe, two-man saw, electric saw, or natural causes, and which direction the tree fell even if it is no longer there. Other discoveries may be made such as the species of tree, if the tree was cut down on a windy day, and sometimes even whether the tree was felled on a cold or comparatively warm day! For a more detailed study of this activity see "Stump Scouting" in William G. Vinal's book *Nature Recreation.*

Animal baiting. A spot is chosen in a natural area and a piece of meat or fish placed under a small log. Loose soil is scattered around and smoothed out. Students return to the same spot the next day. Animal tracks leading to the bait are often discovered; plaster casts may be made of them and taken back to the classroom for identification purposes. A variety of insects will probably have been attracted to the bait and can be taken for a permanent collection. In place of food, a salt lick may be used to attract deer and other mammals.

Soil erosion and soil control demonstration. Four separate areas are marked off, each roughly five feet by fifteen feet, on a plot of land that has some incline. On one such area, the vegetation is completely removed. On the second area, a good covering of vegetation is left. Terraces are constructed and crops planted on the third area and strip crops are developed on the fourth. A catch basin is constructed at the foot of each area for the run-off water. This water is later collected to determine the amount of soil lost from each area after a rain. Observations of the conditions of the soil are also made to determine the effectiveness of the various methods of planting crops.

The quadrat ecology study. The quadrat ecology activity is similar to "Nature by the Square Yard" except it is a more extensive study, usually accomplished in conjunction with a high school science class. It involves staking or measuring out a plot of land, the size determined by the organisms being studied. The next procedure is to observe and to record all living organisms found within the area. Diggings are also made to uncover forms of life which live under the soil. Although larger forms of animals may not be observed, other evidence of their presence might be found, such as animal droppings (a method of identifying specific species of animals), tracks, gnawings, dust baths, and nests. In the large quadrat there are opportunities to delve into such studies as plant succession, and the interdependence of both large and small organisms to each other and to man.[1]

Weather station. Forecasting the weather accurately with the use of instruments appeals to many students. Reading and interpreting weather instruments is an excellent introduction to the study of meteorology and climatology. Crude but fairly good weather instruments can be made by the students, or instruments can be purchased. Weather forecasting includes the use of such measuring instruments as a barometer, hygrometer, anemometer, rain gauge, and high-low thermometer. The noting of wind velocity, wind direction, and humidity, and observation of the variety of cloud formations and their interpretation are also part of forecasting. The study of weather is often related to its effect on animals, plant life, and the physical earth.

There are literally hundreds of other activities and projects which have been made a part of school-conducted outdoor education

[1] Robert E. Brown, "The Quadrat: An Approach To The Study of Ecology," *Manual For Outdoor Laboratories* (Danville, Illinois: Interstate Printers and Publishers, Inc., 1959), pp. 55–57.

programs, and there are a number of fine books which describe them. Space does not permit the authors to do much more than present a sampling of some of the activities which are being conducted by schools throughout the country:

ACTIVITIES INVOLVING OUTDOOR LIVING SKILLS

- Use of compass—orienteering
- Map reading
- Fire building and safety
- Outdoor cooking
- Fishing
- First aid
- Selection of proper wood for various campcraft activities
- Use of knife, hatchet, axe
- Hunting—bow and arrow, rifle—safety
- Survival techniques—living off the land
- Construction of outdoor shelters
- Interpreting nature's signs

NATURAL SCIENCE AND CONSERVATION ACTIVITIES

Observations:

- Soil erosion (water and wind)
- Chemical weathering of rocks and trees
- Weather
- Pine plantation
- Birds
- Water pollution and how it has affected the local area
- Mammals
- Amphibians
- Reptiles
- Insects
- Seasonal changes in a forest
- Types of vegetation on a slope at different elevations
- Adopt a tree and keep a diary of it for a class term, observing changes in the tree and animals that visit it

Collections:

- Rock and minerals
- Different soils
- Fossils
- Seashells and fresh water shells
- Seaweed
- Seeds
- Leaves
- Twigs
- Insects
- Birds' nests (last year's)

Studies:

- Animal behavior
- Edible plants
- Poisonous plants
- Astronomy—effect of the moon & sun on bodies of water, constellations, light years
- Identification of plants
- Identification of birds' nests
- Identification of animals and their tracks
- Identification of calls and songs of animals (recordings available)
- Transpiration
- How green plants produce food (photosynthesis)
- Symbiosis (two different organisms living together)
- Parasitism

Seeds (means of dispersement)
Rocks and minerals (splitting open and studying with a hand lens)
Plant folklore
Ecology (relationship of plants and animals to their environment)
Effects of misuse of natural resources

Doing:

Plantings of grass, shrubs, and trees (to control erosion, provide food and cover for wildlife, beautification)
Bird banding (Federal license required)
Soil tests
Growing plants from cuttings
A tree and animal census of a local area to determine variety and number of species; live-trap and tag the animals
Surveying
Gardening (vegetable and herbs)
Pruning, thinning, and selective cutting of forest trees
Embed insects and plants in plastic for a permanent collection
Moonlight hikes
Nature photography (flowers, star and moon trails, animals)
Animal baiting (to study animal tracks)

Constructing:

Check dams
Animal shelters (bird houses, brush piles)
Nature electric quiz boards
A bird blind (for observing and photographing birds)
Bird feeders
Cages (temporary homes for wildlife)
Nature trail and nature trail signs
Riprapping (control and prevent soil erosion)
Small outdoor zoo
Fire breaks
Demonstration models depicting conservation principles
Live animal traps
Bridges

Making:

Plaster casts of animal tracks and leaves
Herbariums (mounted collection of pressed, dried plants)
Terrariums and aquariums depicting plants and animals indigenous to the local area
Crafts, such as rustic jewelry, made from natural materials
Spore prints
Graftings of plants
Maple syrup (tapping maple trees)
Leaf prints (spatter, crayon, ozalid prints, and blueprints)
Dyes from plants
Weather instruments

Visiting:

- Abandoned farm
- Modern dairy farm
- Fish hatchery
- Flood control dam
- Agricultural experimental station
- Reservoir
- Water purification plant
- Sewage disposal plant
- Abandoned lumber camp

Outdoor Recreation Activities

Although the emphasis in a number of chapters has been upon natural history and conservation, and how these areas can be integrated with the curriculum, there are other activities of a more recreational nature which should be considered in outdoor education. More educators are beginning to realize that schools also have the responsibility for education for leisure. Such education must start early both in and out of schools.

Justification for including more outdoor recreational-type activities in the school curriculum is that schools should have a responsibility for the safety of its students, in and out of class. As a result of a tremendous upsurge in outdoor sports such as boating, fishing, hunting, and skiing, there has been a corresponding increase in the number of accidents. The increase in the accident rate is primarily the result of lack of essential knowledge of a particular sport by the people who engage in it. Hunters unfamiliar not only with their weapons and the safety factors involved, but with the behavior of the animals they are hunting—people ignorant of the boating rules and uninstructed in the proper handling and behavior of their boats—these are serious problems which should be the concern of school systems at all levels.

The various outdoor education workshops held periodically throughout the country cover in their programs many of the recreational type activities along with science and conservation. Following is a listing of recreational activities from a typical program conducted by the New England Outdoor Education Workshop in collaboration with the National Outdoor Education Project of the AAHPER at Sargent Camp (Sargent College, Boston University) in Peterborough, New Hampshire:

Archery:

- History of archery
- Target and field archery techniques (including safety precautions)
- Systems of sighting or aiming

Teaching methods and materials
How to hunt with a bow

Fly Tying:
Materials used
Making of bucktails, streamers, wet and dry flies, bugs
Rod winding
Purpose of fly tying (recreation, encourage proper use of natural resources, encourage off-street activity)

Mountain Climbing:
How mountain climbing ties in with educational activities (philosophy—applications)
Demonstration of hiking and climbing equipment
Hunting—camping relationship

Snow Skiing:
Purpose and Objectives
A. Physical development and fitness
B. Recreation and competitive skiing
C. Commercial values of skiing
D. Administration of school program (area to be used, transportation, instruction, how to finance)
E. Equipment
F. Organized skiing (description of the various ski organizations)
G. Films

Canoe and Boat Handling for Fishermen, Hunters, and Small Craft Operators:
Differences in handling of boats and canoes (characteristics of each)
Boats and canoes—how to launch and enter
Canoes—how to carry, balance, paddle, and care for
Outboard motors on canoes and boats
Using boats and canoes for shelter
Techniques of towing canoes and boats

Other outdoor education workshops include Family Camping in their programs, for this activity has become popular in recent years. Those concerned about saving natural outdoor areas for fishing, boating, hunting, and educational activities must direct their attention to family campers, for with other outdoor sport enthusiasts they make up a sizeable voting public who will help determine the fate of our wilderness and semi-wilderness areas. If they have a bad camping experience they may be unconcerned about the destiny of outdoor America. Should super highways, megalopolises, and the like, replace our outdoors, educators will lose forever a vital tool in the educational process whose potential they are just beginning to recognize. In addition, the American people may well lose a vital segment of their spiritual makeup which evolved from living closely with the earth, and which gave birth to the rugged individual and to the American pioneering spirit.

It has been seen in this chapter that there are many activities and projects which can be incorporated into an outdoor education program. The list presented and described here by no means exhausts all of the potential activities which can be conducted when the whole outdoors serves as the classroom. Indeed, the number of activities which can be developed is limited primarily by the knowledge and imagination of the teachers responsible for the program.

Obviously, not all of the activities mentioned in this chapter will have the same educational value for all classes, nor, for that matter, for each individual within a given class. This, of course, is how it should be. Some activities and projects are more challenging than others and should be handled by those students who have the potential abilities to cope with them. Less difficult activities and projects can be given to those students who may become more easily discouraged.

Due to the extensive range and educational levels of outdoor education activities and projects, the authors are convinced, as a result of personal observations and experiences, that there are relatively few programs which can have so many advantageous effects upon a child whether he be exceptional, of average intelligence, retarded, handicapped, or even have tendencies toward juvenile delinquency.

Bibliography

American Association for Health, Physical Education, and Recreation, *Children in Focus,* 1954 Yearbook. Washington, D.C.: AAHPER, 1954.

———, *Outdoor Education for American Youth.* Washington, D.C.: AAHPER, 1957.

American Association of School Administrators, *Conservation—In The People's Hands.* Washington, D.C.: AASA Commission on Conservation, 1964.

Bale, R. O., *Conservation for Camp and Classroom.* Minneapolis, Minn.: Burgess Publishing Co., 1962.

———, *Outdoor Living.* Minneapolis, Minn.: Burgess Publishing Co., 1961.

Bathhurst, Effie G. and Hill, Wilhelmina, U.S. Department of Health, Education, and Welfare, Office of Education, *Conservation Experiences for Children,* Bulletin 1957, No. 16.

Berger, Jean H., *A Plan for Developing Competencies for Leadership In School Camping and Outdoor Education for Elementary Education Students.* Unpublished doctoral thesis, New York University, 1958.

Brightbill, Charles K., *Man and Leisure.* Englewood Cliffs, N.J.: Prentice-Hall, Inc., 1960.

Brown, Albert W., "The Academic Aspect of Outdoor Education," *Extending Education,* VI, No. 1, September 1961.

Brown, Jean G., *Job Description and Qualifications for Camp Leadership Positions.* Unpublished doctoral thesis, New York University, 1958.

Brown, Robert E., and Mouser, G. W., *Techniques for Teaching Conservation Education.* Minneapolis, Minn.: Burgess Publishing Co., 1964.

Burns, Gerald P., *Program of the Modern Camp.* Englewood Cliffs, N.J.: Prentice-Hall, Inc., 1954.

Campbell, Sam, *Nature's Messages.* Chicago, Illinois: Rand McNally & Co., 1952.

Carlson, Reynold E., "Enriching the School Curriculum," *The Bulletin of the National Association of Secondary School Principals,* May 1947.

Chamberlin, Dean and Enid, Drought, N. E., and Scott, W. E., *Did They Succeed in College?* New York: Harper & Row, Publishers, 1942.

Clarke, James Mitchell, *Public School Camping.* Stanford, California: Stanford University Press, 1951.

Clawson, Marion and others, *Future Land Use in the United States.* Resources for the Future, Washington, D.C., 1963.

Conservation Education in American Schools, 29th Yearbook. Washington, D.C.: American Association of School Administrators, 1951.

Department of Elementary School Principals, "Camping Education for the Elementary Child," *The National Elementary Principal*, XXVIII, No. 4, February 1949.

Donaldson, George W., *School Camping*. New York: Association Press, 1952.

Educational Policies Commission, *The Central Purpose of American Education*. Washington, D.C.: National Education Association, 1961.

———, *Education For All American Youth*. Washington, D.C.: National Education Association, 1952.

Extending Education Through Camping. New York: Life Camps, Inc., 1948.

Freeberg, William H., and Taylor, Loren E., *Philosophy of Outdoor Education*. Minneapolis, Minn.: Burgess Publishing Co., 1961.

———, *Programs In Outdoor Education*. Minneapolis, Minn.: Burgess Publishing Co., 1963.

Freit, Edwin L., and Peterson, Del G., *Design for Outdoor Education*. Yakima, Washington: P. S. Printers, Inc., 1956.

Gabrielsen, M. Alexander, and Miles, Caswell M., *Sports and Recreation Facilities for School and Community*. Englewood Cliffs, N.J.: Prentice-Hall, Inc., 1958.

Gabrielsen, M. Alexander, Spears, Betty, and Gabrielsen, B. W., *Aquatic Handbook*. Englewood Cliffs, N.J.: Prentice-Hall, Inc., 1961.

Galbreath, J. W., "The Value of a Nature Area in Teaching Biology and Conservation," *Illinois Educational Press Bulletin*, March 1960.

Gilliland, John W., *A Study of the Administrative Factors in Establishing a Program of School Camping*. Unpublished doctoral thesis, New York University, 1949.

———, *School Camping*. Washington, D.C.: National Education Association, Department of Supervision and Curriculum Development, 1954.

Hamm, Russell L., and Hason, Larry, *An Ecological Approach to Conservation*. Minneapolis, Minn.: Burgess Publishing Co., 1964.

Hammerman, Donald R., and William M., *Teaching in the Outdoors*. New York, N.Y.: Recreation Book Center, 1962.

Hammett, Catherine T., and Musselman, Virginia, *The Camp Program Book*. New York: Association Press, 1951.

Hillcourt, William, *Field Book of Nature Activities*. New York: G. P. Putnam's Sons, 1950.

Holland, Kenneth, and Beckel, George L., *Work Camps for High School Youth*. Washington, D.C.: American Council on Education prepared for the American Youth Commission, 1941.

Irwin, Frank L., *The Theory of Camping*. New York: A. S. Barnes & Co., 1950.

Jaeger, Ellsworth, *Wildwood Wisdom*. New York: The Macmillan Company, 1957.

Jersild, Arthur T., and others, "A Further Comparison of Pupils in 'Activity' and 'Non-Activity' Schools," *Journal of Experimental Education*, ix (1941).

Kelley, Earl, *In Defense of Youth*. Englewood Cliffs, N.J.: Prentice-Hall, Inc., 1962.

———, *Education for What is Real.* New York: Harper & Row, Publishers, 1947.

Kieran, John, *A Natural History of New York.* New York: Houghton Mifflin Company, 1959.

Kirk, John J., "An Analysis of State Laws Affecting the Operation of Children's Summer Camps in the United States, with a Suggested Universal Legislation Program." Unpublished doctoral thesis, University of Michigan, 1963.

Koopman, Robert G., *My Town.* East Lansing, Michigan: March 1956.

Kleindienst, Viola K., "A Study of the Experiences of Camping for the Purpose of Pointing Out Ways in Which a School Camp Program May Supplement the Elementary School at the Sixth Grade Level." Unpublished doctoral thesis, New York University, 1957.

Leisure in America: Blessing or Curse. Monograph 4 in a series by the American Academy of Political and Social Science. Philadelphia, Pa.: April 1964.

Leopold, Aldo, *A Sand County Almanac and Sketches Here and There.* New York: Oxford University Press, 1949.

MacMillan, Dorothy Lou, *School Camping and Outdoor Education.* Dubuque, Iowa: William C. Brown Company, Inc., 1956.

Manley, Helen, and Drury, M. F., *Education Through School Camping.* St. Louis, Mo.: The C. V. Mosby Company, 1952.

Mason, Bernard S., *Camping and Education.* New York: McCall Co., 1930.

McBride, Robert, *Camping in the Mid Century.* Bradford Woods, Indiana: American Camping Association, 1953.

McKnight, Martha E., "Contributions and Potentialities of School Camping." Unpublished doctoral thesis, Columbia University, 1952.

Miracle, Leonard, with Decker, Maurice H., *Complete Book of Camping.* New York: Outdoor Life, Harper & Row, Publishers, 1961.

Nash, J. B., *Philosophy of Recreation and Leisure.* Dubuque, Iowa: William C. Brown Company, Inc., 1953.

———, *Recreation: Pertinent Readings.* Dubuque, Iowa: William C. Brown Company, Inc., 1965.

Nash, Roderick W., *Wilderness and the American Mind.* Unpublished doctoral thesis, University of Wisconsin, 1964.

National Association of Biology Teachers, Richard L. Weaver, ed., *Manual for Outdoor Laboratories.* Danville, Ill.: The Interstate Printers and Publishers, Inc., 1959.

———, *Handbook for Teaching Conservation and Resource Use.* Danville, Ill.: The Interstate Printers and Publishers, Inc., 1958.

Nickelsburg, Janet, *The Nature Program at Camp.* Minneapolis, Minn.: Burgess Publishing Co., 1960.

Outdoor Recreation for America. A report to the President and to the Congress of the Outdoor Recreation Resources Review Commission, includes 27 supplemental reports. Washington, D.C.: U.S. Government Printing Office, January 1962.

Peterson, Gunnar A., & Edgren, Harry D., *Outdoor Winter Activities.* New York: Association Press, 1962.

Pepper, Nathan H., "A Study of School Camping with Special Emphasis on Program, Objectives, Curriculum, Administration, and Evaluation." Unpublished thesis, University of Houston, 1952.

Physical Education and Recreation Series, "School Camping and Outdoor Education," *Bulletin,* University of the State of New York, Albany, May 1950, 25.

Sells, Saul B., Loftus, John J., and Herbert, Louis, "Evaluative Studies of the Activity Program in the New York City Public Schools: A Preliminary Report," *Journal of Experimental Education,* O (1941).

Sharp, L. B., "Basic Considerations in Outdoor and Camping Education." The Bulletin of the *National Association of Secondary School Principals,* May 1947.

———, "Camping and Outdoor Education," *National Education Association Journal,* May 1947.

———, "The Place of Outdoor Education in the Education of Children," *Education,* LXXIII, September 1952.

Smith, Julian W., *Outdoor Education.* Washington, D.C.: AAHPER, 1956.

Smith, Julian W., Carlson, Reynold E., Donaldson, George W., and Masters, Hugh B., *Outdoor Education.* Englewood Cliffs, N.J.: Prentice-Hall, Inc., 1963.

Smith, Stanley, and Shores, *Fundamentals of Curriculum Development.* Yonkers on Hudson, N.Y.: World Book Co., 1950.

Stapp, William B., *Integrating Outdoor and Conservation Education Into the Curriculum.* Minneapolis, Minn.: Burgess Publishing Co., 1964.

Thurston, Lee M., *Community School Camp.* Lansing, Michigan: Department of Public Instruction, 1950.

———, *Youth Love Thy Woods and Templed Hills.* Lansing, Michigan: Department of Public Instruction, 1949.

Treat, Dorothy A., "City Nature," *Audubon Nature Bulletin.* New York: National Audubon Society, 1955.

Trillingham, C. C., *Outdoor Education: A Handbook For School Districts.* Los Angeles, California: Office of the Superintendent of Schools, 1954.

Vinal, William Gould, *Nature Recreation.* New York: McGraw-Hill Book Company, Inc., 1940.

Weiss, Irving J., "Enriching Science Through Outdoor Education." A Resource Guide for Teaching the Use of the Park in the Elementary Schools. Unpublished doctoral thesis, New York University, 1961.

Wenrich, Esther M., "The Staffing of Public Elementary School Camps." Unpublished thesis, Columbia University, 1955.

Wilcox, Arthur T., ed., *Outdoor Education—A Way to Better Living,* Park Management Bulletin No. 6. East Lansing, Michigan: Michigan State University Press, 1957.

Wrightstone, Jacob W., *Appraisals of New Elementary School Practices.* New York: Bureau of Publications, Teachers College, Columbia University, 1938.

Wylie, James A., "Camping and Outdoor Schools," *Education,* LXXIII, No. 1, September 1952.

Appendix

Sources of Information

There are numerous sources of information on outdoor education subjects as well as on outdoor recreation.[1] The agencies listed below have been classified according to their auspices.

FEDERAL AGENCIES

The Bureau of Outdoor Recreation: Department of the Interior, Washington, D.C., 20240. Can advise on a wide range of outdoor recreation matters including most problems in state, county, and regional outdoor recreation programs.

The Soil Conservation Service: Department of Agriculture, Washington, D.C., 20250. Provides technical and financial assistance for recreation development at watershed protection projects, and technical assistance for converting cropland to recreation use and for developing outdoor recreation facilities as a source of income for rural landowners.

The Urban Renewal Administration: Housing and Home Finance Agency, Washington, D.C., 20410. Makes cost sharing grants and loans to help state and local governments acquire land in urban areas for preservation as open space, prepare comprehensive land-use plans, and redevelop blighted or slum areas.

Bureau of Indian Affairs: U.S. Department of the Interior, Washington, D.C., 20240. Assists Indian tribes in establishing tourist attractions and outdoor recreation developments on tribal land.

Bureau of Land Management: U.S. Department of the Interior, Washington, D.C., 20240. Provides for acquisition of certain Federal lands by qualified nonprofit organizations, state, and local governments for recreation use.

National Park Service: U.S. Department of the Interior, Washington, D.C., 20240. Operates all national parks. Provides technical services upon request and has a number of publications which provide planning assistance.

Bureau of Reclamation: U.S. Department of the Interior, Washington, D.C., 20240. Its general policy is to transfer reservoir and other projects areas having recreational value to other Federal, state, or local government agencies for the development and administration of recreation resources.

[1] Most of the agencies listed have publications; some have instructional motion pictures or film strips.

Bureau of Sport Fisheries and Wildlife: U.S. Department of the Interior, Washington, D.C., 20240. Provides information to states and local communities on all aspects of fish and wildlife management. Conducts research and training programs.

Federal Extension Service: U.S. Department of Agriculture, Washington, D.C., 20250. Works through the State Extension Services, which are a part of the Land Grant University System to provide educational assistance and advice to farmers and landowners regarding the development of income-producing recreation enterprises on private-owned and other non-Federal lands.

Farmers Home Administration: U.S. Department of Agriculture, Washington, D.C., 20250. Makes loans to individual farmers who are unable to get needed credit elsewhere for development of income-producing outdoor recreation enterprises.

The Forest Service: U.S. Department of Agriculture, Washington, D.C., 20250. Is responsible for the development and administration of public recreation facilities within the National Forest. They manage the largest land area in the country.

Army Corps of Engineers: U.S. Department of Defense, Washington, D.C. It controls the rivers and harbors of the United States.

Housing and Home Finance Agency: Washington, D.C. Has an open space land program which provides grants to states and local public agencies for the acquisition of land in urban and urbanizing areas for park, recreation, conservation, science, or historic purposes.

Tennessee Valley Authority: Knoxville, Tennessee. A resource development agency, primarily concerned with flood control, electric power, and river navigation. However, one of the major byproducts of their work is the establishment of great water resource areas which have considerable recreation value.

STATE AGENCIES

Each state will differ somewhat in agency organization. Most states have departments of conservation and commerce which are likely to have information related to outdoor education and recreation.

PRIVATE ORGANIZATIONS

Many additional national, regional, and state citizen and professional organizations, in outdoor recreation and related fields, are listed in *Conservation Directory,* published annually by the National Wildlife Federation, 1412 Sixteenth St., N.W., Washington, D.C., 20036. Cost: $1.

American Automobile Association: 1712 G. St., N.W., Washington, D.C., 20006. Interests include improved highway billboard controls and scenic highways. Roadside Councils, active in a number of states, may be contacted through the AAA or its state affiliates.

American Camping Association: Bradford Woods, Bloomington, Indiana. National professional organization in camping. Has numerous publications. Send for listing.

American Forestry Association: 919 17th St., N.W., Washington, D.C., 20006. A membership organization "for advancement of intelligent management and use of forests and related resources."

American Forest Products Industries, Inc.: 1816 N. St., N.W., Washington 6, D.C.

American Nature Association: 1214 16th St., N.W., Washington 6, D.C.

American Planning and Civic Association: 901 Union Trust Building, Washington, D.C., 20005. A membership organization dedicated to understanding of planning for best use of land and other natural resources.

Bituminous Coal Institute: 1425 H. Street, N.W., Washington, D.C.

Boy Scouts of America: National Council, New Brunswick, N.J.

Camp Fire Girls, Inc.: 16 East 48th St., N.Y. 17, N.Y.

Conservation Education Association: Selected references on conservation education for teachers and pupils. 15¢. Billings, Montana.

The Conservation Foundation: 30 East 40th St., N.Y. 16, N.Y.

The Garden Club of America: 15 East 58th St., N.Y. 22, N.Y.

Girl Scouts of the United States of America: 155 East 44th St., N.Y. 17, N.Y.

Izaak Walton League of America: 1326 Waukegan Road, Glenview, Ill., 60025. A membership organization with local chapters; also direct national memberships. Promotes conservation and enjoyment of all natural resources with emphasis on outdoor recreation.

National Association of Soil and Water Conservation Districts: 1435 G. St., N.W., Washington, D.C., 20005. An organization of local soil and water conservation districts.

National Audubon Society: 1130 Fifth Ave., New York, N.Y., 10028. A membership organization with local units dedicated to conservation of wildlife and other natural resources. Its Nature Centers Division provides guidance on planning and operation of community nature centers.

National Conference on State Parks: 901 Union Trust Building, Washington, D.C., 20005. A membership organization "to foster research, planning, acquisition, development, conservation, and use of state parks and related types of recreation resources."

National Education Association: 1201 16th St., N.W., Washington 6, D.C.

National Geographic Society: 16th and M. Sts., N.W., Washington 6, D.C.

National Parks Association: 1300 New Hampshire Avenue, N.W., Washington, D.C., 20036. A membership organization. Purposes include protection of the national parks and monuments and national forests.

National Recreation Association: 8 W. Eighth St., New York, N.Y., 10011. A membership organization which provides a wide range of urban-oriented services, including planning surveys for local governments.

National Wildlife Federation: 1412 Sixteenth St., N.W., Washington, D.C., 20036. A federation of state wildlife and conservation organizations; also has direct national memberships. For the wise use of wildlife and other natural resources.

The Nature Conservancy: 2039 K. St., N.W., Washington, D.C., 20006. A membership organization with local units dedicated to the preservation of natural areas for scientific and educational purposes.

Outboard Boating Club of America: 307 N. Michigan Ave., Chicago, Ill., 60601. A trade association with local boating club affiliates. Promotes the interests of those who use boats for recreation.

Sierra Club: 1950 Mills Tower, San Francisco, California, 94104. A national membership organization with local chapters. "To explore, enjoy, and protect national scenic resources."

Sport Fishing Institute: Bond Building, Washington, D.C., 20005. An industry-supported educational and scientific organization "to improve sport fishing through fish conservation research, education, and service."

The Wilderness Society: 2144 P. St., N.W., Washington, D.C., 20037. A membership organization "to secure the preservation of wilderness. . . ."

Wildlife Management Institute: 709 Wire Building, Washington, D.C., 20005. An educational organization supported by manufacturers of sporting arms and ammunition to promote better use of natural resources.

Index

U

V

W

Y